LEARNING ADVENTURES
IN MATH
Grades 5–6

By the Staff of Score@Kaplan

Foreword by Alan Tripp

Simon & Schuster

**This series is dedicated to our
Score@Kaplan parents and children—
thank you for making these books possible.**

Published by
Kaplan Educational Centers and Simon & Schuster
1230 Avenue of the Americas
New York, NY 10020

Special thanks to: Elissa Grayer, Doreen Beauregard, Julie Schmidt, Rebecca Geller
Schwartz, Linda Lott, Janet Cassidy, Marlene Greil, Nancy McDonald, Sarah Jane
Bryan, Chris Wilsdon, Janet Montal, Jeannette Sanderson, David Stienecker, Dan
Greenberg, Kathy Wilmore, Dorrie Berkowitz, Brent Gallenberger, and Molly Walsh

Head Coach and General Manager, Score@Kaplan: Alan Tripp
President, Score@Kaplan: Robert L. Waldron
Series Content and Development: Mega-Books
Project Editor: Mary Pearce
Production Editor: Donna Mackay, Graphic Circle Inc.
Art Director: Elana Goren-Totino
Illustrators: Rick Brown, Ryan Brown, Sandy Forrest, Larry Nolte,
Evan Polenghi, Fred Schrier, Peter Spacek, Arnie Ten
Cover Design: Cheung Tai
Cover Photograph: Michael Britto

Manufactured in the United States of America
Published Simultaneously in Canada

January 1998
10 9 8 7 6 5 4 3 2 1

ISBN:0-684-84436-2

Contents

Note to Parents. iv
Note to Kids vi

Grade Five

Numeration 1
Computation 6
Geometry 8
Measurement 13
Fractions 15
Decimals 21
Percent 24
Ratios 26
Proportion 27
Graphing 28
Probability 30
Problem Solving 31
Algebra 32

Grade Six

Numeration 33
Computation 34
Geometry 37
Measurement 44
Fractions 46
Decimals 49
Percent 52
Ratios 54
Scale. 55
Coordinate Geometry. 56
Graphing 57
Probability 58
Problem Solving 60
Algebra 63

Puzzle. 64
Answers. 65
How Do You Foster Your Child's Interest in Learning? 71

Dear Parents,

Your child's success in school is important to you, and at Score@Kaplan we are always pleased when the kids who attend our educational centers do well on their report cards. But what we really want for our kids is not just good grades. We also want everything that good grades are supposed to represent:

- We want our kids to master the key communication systems that make civilization possible: language (spoken and written), math, the visual arts, and music.
- We want them to build their critical-thinking skills so they can understand, appreciate, and improve their world.
- We want them to continually increase their knowledge and to value learning as the key to a happy, successful life.
- We want them to always do their best, to persist when challenged, to be a force for good, and to help others whenever they can.

These are ambitious goals, but our children deserve no less. We at Score@Kaplan have already helped thousands of children across the country in our centers, and we hope this series of books for children in first through sixth grades will reach many more households.

Simple Principles

We owe the remarkable success of Score@Kaplan to a few simple principles. This book was developed with these principles in mind.

- We expect every child to succeed.
- We make it possible for every child to succeed.
- We reinforce every instance of success, no matter how small.

Assessing Your Child

One helpful approach in assessing your child's skills is to ask yourself the following questions.

- How much is my child reading? At what level of difficulty?
- Has my child mastered appropriate language arts skills, such as spelling, grammar, and syntax?
- Does my child have the ability to express appropriately complex thoughts when speaking or writing?
- Does my child demonstrate mastery of all age-appropriate math skills, such as mastery of addition and subtraction facts, multiplication tables, division rules, and so on?

These questions are a good starting place and may give you new insights into your child's academic situation.

What's Going on at School

Parents will always need to monitor the situation at school and take responsibility for their child's learning. You should find out what your child should be learning at each grade level and match that against what your child actually learns.

The activity pages in *Learning Adventures* were developed using the standards developed by the professional teachers associations. As your child explores the activities in *Learning Adventures*, you might find that a particular concept hasn't been taught in school or hasn't yet been mastered by your child. This presents a great opportunity for both of you. Together you can learn something new.

Encouraging Your Child to Learn at Home

This book is full of fun learning activities you can do with your child to build understanding of key concepts in language arts, math, and science. Most activities are designed for your child to do independently. But, that doesn't mean that you can't work on them together or invite your child to share the work with you. As you help your child learn, please bear in mind the following observations drawn from experience in our centers:

- Positive reinforcement is the key. Try to maintain a ratio of at least five positive remarks to every negative one.
- All praise must be genuine. Try praises such as: "That was a good try," "You got this part of it right," or "I'm proud of you for doing your best, even though it was hard."
- When a child gets stuck, giving the answer is often not the most efficient way to help. Ask open-ended questions, or rephrase the problem.
- Remember to be patient and supportive. Children need to learn that hard work pays off.

There's More to Life Than Academic Learning

Most parents recognize that academic excellence is just one of the many things they would like to ensure for their children. At Score@Kaplan, we are committed to developing the whole child. These books are designed to emphasize academic skills and critical thinking, as well as provide an opportunity for positive reinforcement and encouragement from you, the parent.

We wish you a successful and rewarding experience as you and your child embark upon this learning adventure together.

Alan Tripp
General Manager
Score@Kaplan

Dear Kids,

Get your pencils sharpened, and put your game face on! You're about to begin a Learning Adventure. This book is filled with puzzles, games, riddles, and lots of other fun stuff. You can do them alone or with your family and friends. While you're at it, you'll exercise your brain.

If you get stuck on something, look for the Score coaches. Think of them as your personal brain trainers. You can also check your answers on pages 65–70, if you really have to.

We know you'll do a great job. That's why we have a special puzzle inside. After you do three or four pages, you'll see a puzzle piece. Cut it out, then glue it or tape it in place on page 64. When the puzzle is finished, you'll discover a hidden message from us.

So, pump up your mind muscles, and get ready to Score. You'll have a blast and boost your brain power at the same time.

Go for it!

Your Coaches at Score

Big Number Search

You've probably seen some big numbers. Well, what about words that stand for big numbers? Read each word below, and write the number on the line. Then, find and circle that number on the number board. Don't give up! The number may go down, across, diagonally, or backwards.

1. one hundred nine thousand, five hundred sixty-four __109,564__

2. five hundred seventy-eight thousand, three hundred five __578,305__

3. nine hundred thirty-two thousand, two hundred one __932,201__

4. four million, one hundred twenty-nine thousand, four hundred sixty-nine __4,129,469__

5. twelve million, five hundred three thousand, three hundred four __12,503,304__

6. sixty-two million, seven hundred forty-nine thousand, one hundred two __62,749,102__

7. five hundred twelve million, four hundred sixty-nine thousand, seven hundred eighteen __512,469,718__

8. eight hundred thirty-two million, three hundred twenty-seven thousand, one hundred seventy-five __832,327,175__

Remember, commas separate large numbers into groups of three digits.

N	1	5	4	1	0	9	5	6	4	7
U	4	5	7	2	5	6	7	8	1	9
M	1	7	3	5	9	2	8	0	2	1
B	3	1	9	0	6	7	3	5	9	4
E	6	7	5	3	0	7	0	1	4	5
R	1	2	0	3	2	6	5	8	6	9
	5	3	7	0	1	2	6	4	9	3
B	6	2	7	4	9	1	0	2	3	6
O	4	3	6	8	5	9	5	1	2	4
A	6	8	1	7	9	6	4	2	1	5
R										
D										

NAME _____

Juggling Numbers

Justin the Juggler has no trouble at all juggling his
numbers. Ready to try your hand at it? Juggle the digits in
the number cards to make the numbers described below.
The challenge is, you can use a digit only once in a
number. Write the numbers on the line.

You can tell
the size of
a number by
looking at the
place value of
each digit.

1. Make the least number using all the digits. __123,456,789__

2. Make the greatest number using all the digits. __987,654,321__

3. Make the greatest number that is greater than 8,000
   but less than 8,500. __8,498__

4. Make the smallest number that is greater than 35,000
   but less than 36,000. __35,124__

5. Make the greatest number that is greater than 400,000
   but less than 500,000. __498,765__

6. Make the smallest number that is greater than 613,400. __613,425__

7. Make the number that is 50,000 less than 682,471. __632,471__

8. Make the number that is 250,000 less than 373,456. __123,456__

2

NAME_____

Growing Factor Trees

Do you have a green thumb? How about growing some factor trees. Find the product (or answer) planted in each pot. Complete the trees by writing the factors in the empty boxes.

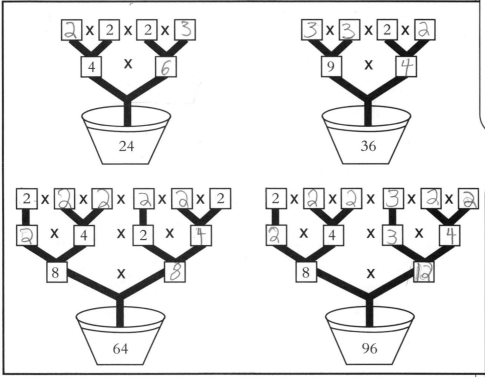

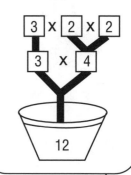

To grow a factor tree, start with the two largest factors. Then keep finding factors until the remaining factors can be divided by only themselves and 1.

All the factors in the last row of branches should equal the product you began with.

Plant factor trees of your own. Pick two products to start with, write them on the pots, and start gardening.

NAME _____

Common Ground

Numbers can have factors in common. Complete these Venn diagrams to find the common factors for each pair of numbers. Then circle the greatest common factor for each pair. One is done for you.

Factors for 18   Factors for 24

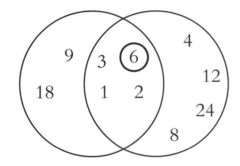

Write the common factors in the space where the circles overlap. Write all the other factors outside the overlapping area.

Factors for 24   Factors for 36

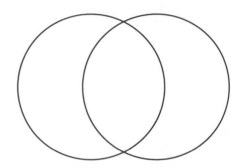

Factors for 8   Factors for 12

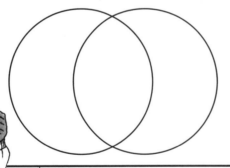

Factors for 16   Factors for 24

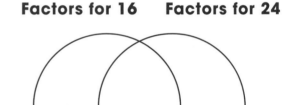

Use the decoder to discover which letters match the greatest common factors you circled. Unscramble the letters to find the answer to this riddle.

Decoder

1 = A	8 = L
3 = S	9 = H
4 = C	10 = W
6 = O	12 = D

What can you keep even after you give it to someone else?

A _____

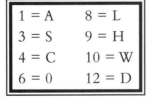

4

Grade 5

NAME_____

Fright Night

What's going on in Freddy's house? He needs some help fast, especially with these ghoulish questions. Read the problems. Use least common multiples to help Freddy find the answers. Write the answers on the lines below. Without you, Freddy doesn't have a ghost of a chance!

1. Freddy hears creaking doors every fourth day. He hears screams every sixth day. He heard them both today. When will he hear creaks and screams at the same time?_____

   doors: multiples of 4: 4, 8, ⑫; screams: multiples of 6: 6, ⑫

   answer: 12 days

2. A goblin pays Freddy a visit every 3 days. A gremlin stops by every 5 days. If Freddy saw them both yesterday, in how many days can he expect to see them together again? _14 days_

   _____

3. Freddy sees strange lights every 8 days. He hears strange voices every 4 days. He smells strange smells every 3 days. Today all three happened. In how many days can he expect this to happen again?

   Fin 24 days

   _____

4. Freddy receives a can of worms every 12 days. Every 15 days a box of bats shows up. Today he found both on his doorstep. How many days will Freddy have before that happens again? _60 More Days_

> To find a least common multiple, write down some multiples of each number. Then look for the smallest number that is a common multiple.

> Now find and cut out the puzzle piece, and glue or tape it in place in the puzzle frame on page 64.

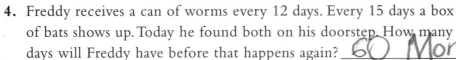

NAME _____

Four Straight

Here's a game you can play with a friend. You'll need 8 playing pieces for each player. Use coins, beans, or anything that will fit on the game board. How to play:

1. The first player picks one number from Number Bank A and one number from Number Bank B.
2. Multiply Number A by Number B. See if you can do it without a calculator. Then check your answer using a calculator.
3. Find the product on the gameboard and place a marker on it.
4. The next player takes a turn.
5. The winner is the first player who has four markers in a row, a column, or on a diagonal.

Number Bank A	
132	426
350	649

Number Bank B	
265	709
597	815

GAMEBOARD

107,580	387,453	285,250	347,190
208,950	302,034	78,804	528,935
171,985	34,980	254,322	248,150
92,750	93,588	112,890	460,141

6

NAME_____

Magic in the Square

Shhhh! Don't tell anyone, but this square is magic. You don't even have to say "Abracadabra" to get it to work. All you have to do is solve the division problems. Then write each remainder in its matching box in the square. When all the boxes in the magic square are filled, add up each row, column, and diagonal, one at a time. What does each one add up to? Write that magic number in the hat.

Great, Master Magician, you found the magic in the square! Now cut out the puzzle piece, and glue or tape it in place in the puzzle frame on page 64.

A. $34\overline{)4,254}$ **B.** $72\overline{)6,561}$ **C.** $327\overline{)7,850}$

D. $532\overline{)6,387}$ **E.** $406\overline{)21,117}$ **F.** $152\overline{)12,015}$

G. $312\overline{)29,960}$ **H.** $617\overline{)12,958}$ **I.** $234\overline{)20,130}$

A.	B.	C.
D.	E.	F.
G.	H.	I.

NAME _____

Shapes and Sides

What's the oldest puzzle in the world? Well, it might be a *tangram,* which was made in China about 4,000 years ago. It's made up of seven pieces called *tans.* The pieces fit together to make different polygons. Cut apart the tans in the left margin and use them to make these polygons. You must use all seven tans to make each shape.

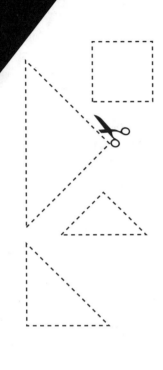

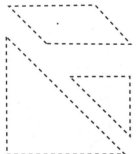

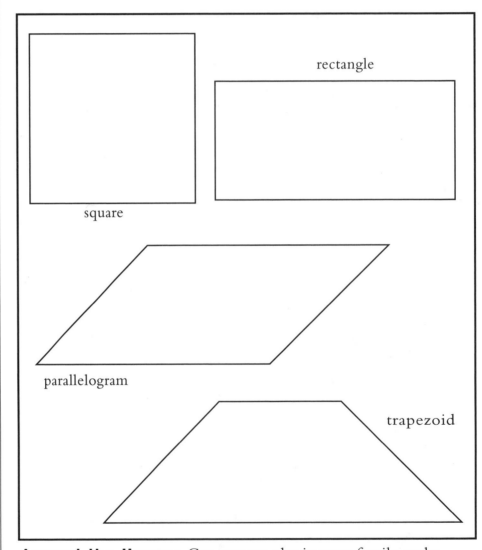

Around the House: Can anyone else in your family make these shapes? Give it a try!

NAME_____

Hexagon Hook-Ups

A *hex* is not always a jinx. Sometimes it's a prefix that means six, like in *hexagon*. Regular hexagons are neat because they can fit together. The more hexagons you have, the more ways you can hook them up. Take a look at these combos, and then try some of your own.

> A regular hexagon has six sides that are the same length and six angles that are the same size.

This is about all you can do with two hexagons.

But with three hexagons, things get a bit more interesting. You can hook them up three different ways.

With four hexagons you can make seven different hookups. Here are two of them.

Use the four hexagons along the side of the page to make five more hexagon hookups. Cut them out. Use them to make different patterns. Draw the patterns you make in the space below.

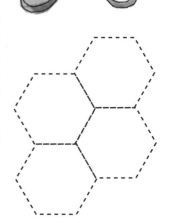

NAME _____

Triangle Teasers

Sometimes you can't believe everything you see. Then you have to look deeper to get the whole story. Use your puzzle skills to find out the whole story about these shapes. Follow the directions below.

1. Here are some triangles inside triangles inside triangles. How many triangles can you find in all? **Hint:** There are more than 20 and fewer than 30.

   _____

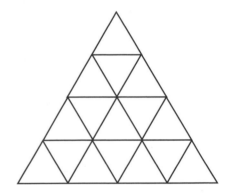

2. This is a square, not a triangle. But here's how you can change that. Trace the square on another sheet of paper. Cut out the square. Then cut along the dotted lines. Put the pieces together to make a triangle.

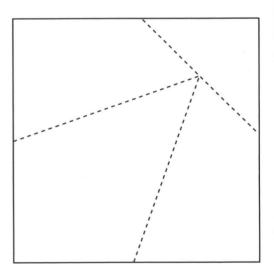

Around the House: Are there puzzle fans in your family? Have them try these.

10

Grade 5

Geometry

Draw lines of
symmetry and symmetrical
figures

NAME

Symmetry = "Sametry"

Are you seeing double? No, you're seeing symmetry. Try
your hand at completing each symmetrical drawing below.
Draw lines on the right side to make a figure that matches
the one on the left. Use the squares on the graph paper
background to help you make each side the same.

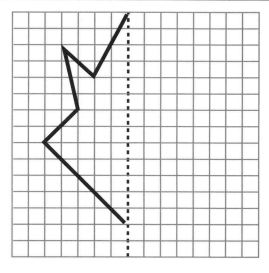

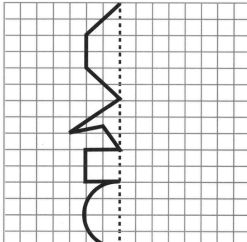

A symmetric figure
is a flat figure
that can be folded
in half so the two
halves match.
Just look at
the symmetric
figure below.

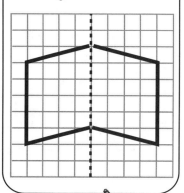

Check Yourself: Count the number and location of squares
each side of the picture used. If they're the same, they're
symmetrical!

NAME _____

Space Figures

A *plane figure*, such as a square, is flat. A *space figure*, such as a cube, is a figure that has volume. If you look at a space figure from different angles, you'll see flat, or plane, figures. Check out the different views of this cone, and then work on the activities below.

cone

bottom view

side view

top view

Play "Name That Space Figure" by yourself or with a friend. Look at the different views of each figure. Write its name on the line. Unscramble the letters next to the line if you need help.

1.

   top view   side view   bottom view

   Name that space figure.
   erindcly _____

2.

   end view   top view   side view

   Name that space figure.
   rreactulang msirp _____

3.

   front view   top view   side view

   Name that space figure.
   asuqre ramidpy _____

NAME_____

Balancing Mobiles

Try your hand at balancing these mobiles. It's really simpler than it looks. All you need to remember is that the weight of the objects times the length of the rod on one side must equal the weight of the objects times the length of the rod on the other side.

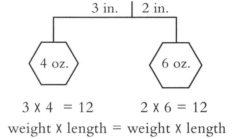

3 in. | 2 in.

4 oz.   6 oz.

$3 \times 4 = 12$ $2 \times 6 = 12$
weight X length = weight X length

That's a great balancing act! Now locate and cut out the puzzle piece on this page. Find where it goes in the puzzle frame on page 64, and glue or tape it in place.

Write in the missing lengths and weights to balance the mobiles.

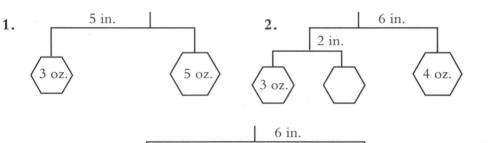

1.   5 in.

3 oz.   5 oz.

2.   6 in.
    2 in.
3 oz.   4 oz.

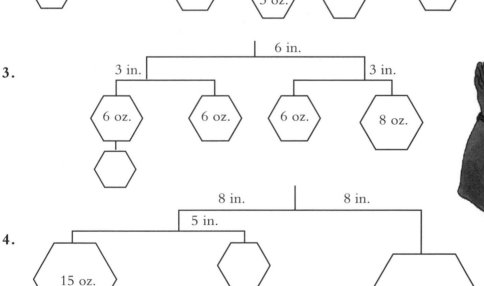

3.   6 in.
    3 in.   3 in.

6 oz.   6 oz.   6 oz.   8 oz.

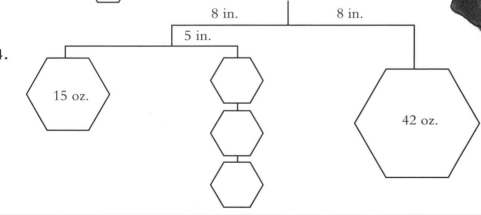

4.   8 in.   8 in.
        5 in.

15 oz.   42 oz.

NAME _____

Surfing the Surface

Surf's up! You can surf around the outside of these figures to find the surface area. Imagine each figure is folded to create a box. Then find the total surface area by keeping track of the areas for each part in the handy "area tables." Then write down the totally awesome total for each figure.

The surface area tells how big the outside of the figure is.
If these figures were folded, they would be rectangular prisms. Picture it!

1.   6 in.

3 in.

2 in.

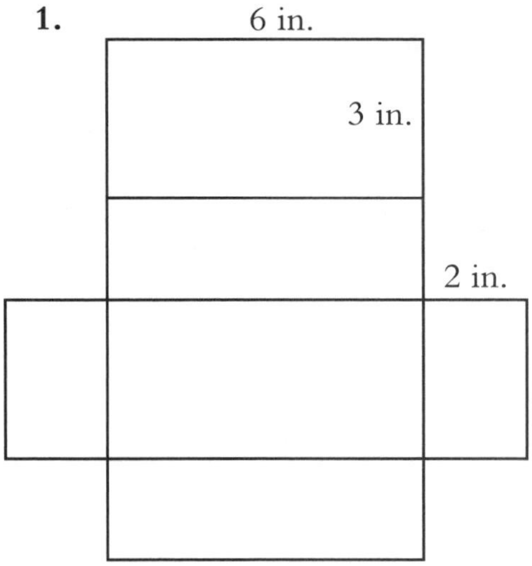

Area Table

Top _____

Bottom _____

Front Side _____

Back Side _____

Left Side _____

Right Side _____

Total Area _____

2.

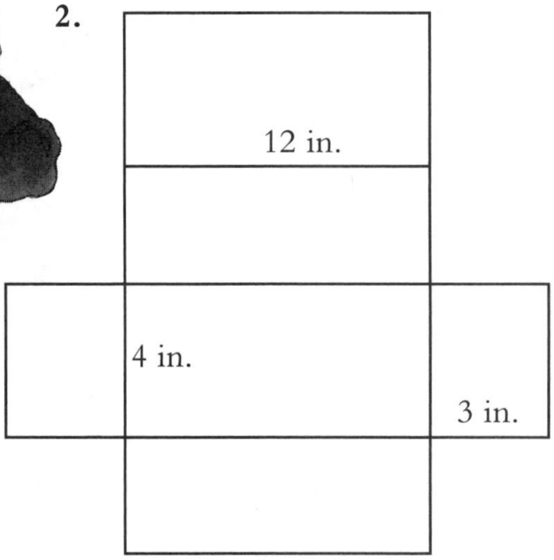

12 in.

4 in.

3 in.

Area Table

Top _____

Bottom _____

Front Side _____

Back Side _____

Left Side _____

Right Side _____

Total Area _____

Fractions
Change impróper fractions
to mixed numbers

NAME_____

South of the Border

Call your travel agent! We're flying to South America on a tour of all the capital cities. By the time you finish this activity, you will know all the capitals in South America. Draw a line to match each improper fraction with the correct mixed number. The matching mixed number matches the capital to the country. (Hint: You may have to reduce more than once.)

1. Argentina	$\frac{11}{6}$	$1\frac{7}{9}$ Quito
2. Bolivia	$\frac{17}{8}$	$2\frac{5}{8}$ Lima
3. Brazil	$\frac{7}{5}$	$2\frac{3}{5}$ Georgetown
4. Chile	$\frac{10}{4}$	$9\frac{1}{2}$ Caracas
5. Colombia	$\frac{21}{12}$	$1\frac{4}{5}$ Asunción
6. Ecuador	$\frac{16}{9}$	$1\frac{2}{5}$ Brasilia
7. Guyana	$\frac{13}{5}$	$1\frac{5}{6}$ Buenos Aires
8. Paraguay	$\frac{18}{10}$	$1\frac{3}{4}$ Bogotá
9. Peru	$\frac{21}{8}$	$2\frac{1}{2}$ Santiago
10. Suriname	$\frac{12}{7}$	$1\frac{5}{7}$ Paramaribo
11. Uruguay	$\frac{24}{9}$	$2\frac{1}{8}$ La Paz
12. Venezuela	$\frac{19}{2}$	$2\frac{2}{3}$ Montevideo

To change an improper fraction to a mixed number, divide the numerator by the denominator.

Now you know your way around South America. ¡Fantástico! Now cut out the puzzle piece, and tape or glue it in place.

Check Yourself: Grab an atlas or a map of South America. Have you matched each capital with the correct country?

NAME _____

Twinkle, Twinkle

Twinkle, twinkle, little star, where are you? There are two
invisible stars inside this picture frame. To find them, all
you have to do is draw straight lines to connect equivalent
fractions. Then color in the stars and make a wish!

Equivalent fractions
are fractions that
name the same
amount.

$\frac{2}{4}$ and $\frac{3}{6}$ are
equivalent
fractions.

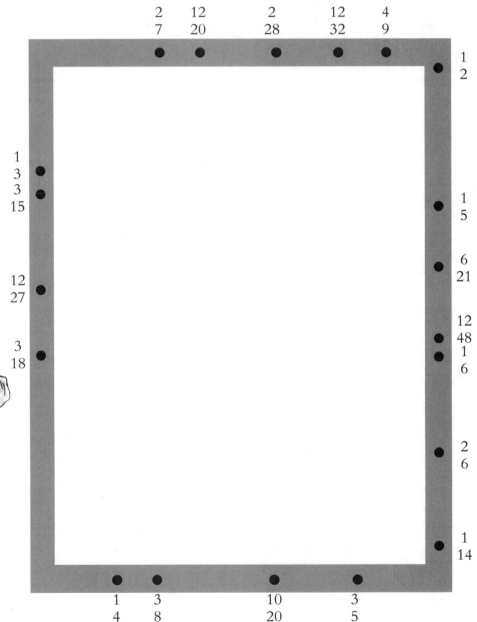

$\frac{2}{7}$ $\frac{12}{20}$ $\frac{2}{28}$ $\frac{12}{32}$ $\frac{4}{9}$

$\frac{1}{2}$

$\frac{1}{3}$
$\frac{3}{15}$

$\frac{12}{27}$

$\frac{3}{18}$

$\frac{1}{5}$

$\frac{6}{21}$

$\frac{12}{48}$
$\frac{1}{6}$

$\frac{2}{6}$

$\frac{1}{14}$

$\frac{1}{4}$ $\frac{3}{8}$ $\frac{10}{20}$ $\frac{3}{5}$

16

Grade 5

NAME_____

Crack the Code

Solve the fraction problems in the Decoder Box. Be sure to
reduce your answers to lowest terms. Then write the letter
that corresponds to each answer above the fraction to solve
the riddles.

Decoder Box		
A. $\dfrac{1}{2} + \dfrac{1}{4} =$ ___	K. $\dfrac{6}{18} + \dfrac{1}{3} =$ ___	R. $\dfrac{7}{10} + \dfrac{2}{5} =$ ___
B. $\dfrac{5}{6} - \dfrac{1}{3} =$ ___	M. $\dfrac{3}{5} - \dfrac{1}{4} =$ ___	S. $\dfrac{4}{5} - \dfrac{1}{3} =$ ___
C. $\dfrac{17}{20} - \dfrac{3}{20} =$ ___	N. $\dfrac{1}{32} + \dfrac{3}{16} =$ ___	T. $\dfrac{3}{8} + \dfrac{1}{2} =$ ___
E. $\dfrac{3}{7} + \dfrac{2}{7} =$ ___	O. $\dfrac{3}{14} + \dfrac{4}{7} =$ ___	U. $\dfrac{11}{12} + \dfrac{1}{4} =$ ___
F. $\dfrac{5}{12} + \dfrac{1}{6} =$ ___	P. $\dfrac{9}{32} + \dfrac{1}{4} =$ ___	W. $\dfrac{8}{10} - \dfrac{1}{2} =$ ___
G. $\dfrac{7}{16} - \dfrac{1}{8} =$ ___	Q. $\dfrac{6}{15} - \dfrac{1}{3} =$ ___	X. $\dfrac{15}{20} - \dfrac{3}{5} =$ ___
I. $\dfrac{6}{10} - \dfrac{4}{20} =$ ___	Y. $\dfrac{13}{15} + \dfrac{2}{3} =$ ___	

1. What are five ducks in a crate called?

$$\overline{\dfrac{3}{4}} \quad \overline{\dfrac{1}{2}} \quad \overline{\dfrac{11}{14}} \quad \overline{\dfrac{3}{20}} \quad \overline{\dfrac{11}{14}} \quad \overline{\dfrac{7}{12}} \quad \overline{\dfrac{1}{15}} \quad \overline{1\dfrac{1}{6}} \quad \overline{\dfrac{3}{4}} \quad \overline{\dfrac{7}{10}} \quad \overline{\dfrac{2}{3}} \quad \overline{\dfrac{5}{7}} \quad \overline{1\dfrac{1}{10}} \quad \overline{\dfrac{7}{15}}$$

2. What is always coming but never arrives?

$$\overline{\dfrac{7}{8}} \quad \overline{\dfrac{11}{14}} \quad \overline{\dfrac{7}{20}} \quad \overline{\dfrac{11}{14}} \quad \overline{1\dfrac{1}{10}} \quad \overline{1\dfrac{1}{10}} \quad \overline{\dfrac{11}{14}} \quad \overline{\dfrac{3}{10}}$$

3. What did the sock say to the foot?

$$\overline{\dfrac{3}{4}} \quad \overline{1\dfrac{1}{10}} \quad \overline{\dfrac{5}{7}} \quad \overline{1\dfrac{8}{15}} \quad \overline{\dfrac{11}{14}} \quad \overline{1\dfrac{1}{6}}$$

$$\overline{\dfrac{17}{32}} \quad \overline{1\dfrac{1}{6}} \quad \overline{\dfrac{7}{8}} \quad \overline{\dfrac{7}{8}} \quad \overline{\dfrac{2}{5}} \quad \overline{\dfrac{7}{32}} \quad \overline{\dfrac{5}{16}} \quad \overline{\dfrac{7}{20}} \quad \overline{\dfrac{5}{7}} \quad \overline{\dfrac{11}{14}} \quad \overline{\dfrac{7}{32}}$$

To add or
subtract fractions
with unlike
denominators,
first make them
equivalent
fractions with
a common
denominator. Then
add or subtract
the numerators.

NAME _____

Card Combos

What a deal! Use the numbers on the cards to make two fractions that result in the sums and products below. Use a number from the cards only once in each set of fractions. Write the fractions in the boxes. The first one is done for you.

1. Sum: $\frac{7}{8}$ **Product:** $\frac{3}{16}$

$$\frac{\boxed{1}}{\boxed{2}} \qquad \frac{\boxed{3}}{\boxed{8}}$$

Here's how we got that:

$$\frac{1}{2} + \frac{3}{8} = \text{(the sum)}$$

$$\frac{1}{2} \times \frac{3}{8} = \text{(the product)}$$

2. Sum: $\frac{13}{20}$ **Product:** $\frac{1}{10}$ **3. Sum:** $\frac{11}{15}$ **Product:** $\frac{2}{15}$

$$\frac{\boxed{}}{\boxed{}} \qquad \frac{\boxed{}}{\boxed{}} \qquad\qquad \frac{\boxed{}}{\boxed{}} \qquad \frac{\boxed{}}{\boxed{}}$$

4. Sum: $\frac{7}{8}$ **Product:** $\frac{3}{32}$ **5. Sum:** $\frac{19}{24}$ **Product:** $\frac{5}{48}$

$$\frac{\boxed{}}{\boxed{}} \qquad \frac{\boxed{}}{\boxed{}} \qquad\qquad \frac{\boxed{}}{\boxed{}} \qquad \frac{\boxed{}}{\boxed{}}$$

6. Sum: $\frac{5}{6}$ **Product:** $\frac{1}{9}$ **7. Sum:** $\frac{11}{10}$ **Product:** $\frac{3}{10}$

$$\frac{\boxed{}}{\boxed{}} \qquad \frac{\boxed{}}{\boxed{}} \qquad\qquad \frac{\boxed{}}{\boxed{}} \qquad \frac{\boxed{}}{\boxed{}}$$

To add fractions, change the fractions so they have a common denominator. Then add the numerators. Reduce if possible. To multiply fractions, multiply the numerators, and then multiply the denominators. Reduce if possible.

NAME_____

Climbing Pyramids

What's the key to climbing these fraction pyramids? The
pharaohs won't tell you, but we will. Start at the bottom.
Multiply the two numbers that are side by side (A **x** B).
Write the product in the box above (C).

Key: A x B = C

1. $2\frac{2}{3}$ x $1\frac{1}{4}$

2. $4\frac{1}{3}$ x $5\frac{1}{2}$

3. $5\frac{3}{8}$ x 4

4. $2\frac{1}{4}$ x $5\frac{1}{3}$

5. 5 x $\frac{2}{5}$ x $\frac{1}{2}$

6. $\frac{1}{5}$ x $2\frac{1}{3}$ x $4\frac{1}{2}$

7. $1\frac{1}{2}$ x $2\frac{1}{3}$ x $2\frac{1}{7}$

8. $\frac{1}{2}$ x $3\frac{1}{2}$ x $\frac{1}{4}$

When you multiply
mixed numbers, first
write the mixed
numbers as improper
fractions.
Then multiply the
fractions. Reduce
them if possible.

NAME _____

Decimal Duel

To change a fraction to a decimal, divide the numerator by the denominator.

Way to go!
Now find the puzzle piece, cut it out, and tape or glue it in place on the puzzle frame on page 64.

For this duel, use your incredibly sharp math skills. You'll also need some markers such as coins or beads. Just follow the directions, and you're all set! Here's what you do:

1. Players take turns.
2. Choose a fraction from the fraction board.
3. Figure out the decimal equivalent to the nearest hundredth.
4. Place your marker in the correct spot on the decimal game board.
5. Cross the fraction off the fraction board.
6. The first player with four markers in a row, column, or diagonal is the winner.

Fraction Board			
$\frac{2}{3}$	$\frac{3}{4}$	$\frac{2}{5}$	$\frac{5}{6}$
$\frac{5}{7}$	$\frac{6}{7}$	$\frac{1}{8}$	$\frac{3}{8}$
$\frac{5}{8}$	$\frac{7}{9}$	$\frac{8}{9}$	$\frac{3}{10}$
$\frac{1}{12}$	$\frac{11}{12}$	$\frac{7}{15}$	$\frac{7}{20}$

Decimal Game Board			
0.66	0.46	0.40	0.08
0.75	0.86	0.13	0.78
0.63	0.38	0.89	0.30
0.83	0.35	0.71	0.92

20

NAME

Look to the Stars

As a member of the Amateur Astronomers Association,
you're an expert on constellation names. For each item,
write the decimals on the lines from least to greatest.
Write the matching letters under the decimals. If
everything is in order, the letters will spell the name
of a constellation.

1.

R — 0.201
O — 0.297
I — 0.232
O — 0.026
N — 0.321

___ ___ ___ ___ ___

2.

G — 0.113
Y — 0.013
C — 0.003
S — 0.333
U — 0.133
N — 0.131

___ ___ ___ ___ ___ ___

3.

G — 0.113
I — 0.378
P — 0.46
B — 0.03
D — 0.312
E — 0.705
P — 0.406
I — 0.103
R — 0.75

___ ___ ___ ___ ___ ___ ___ ___ ___

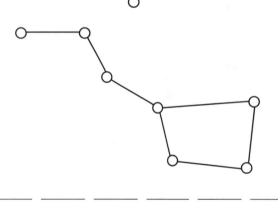

Check Yourself: Use a dictionary to double-check the
constellation names.

NAME _____

Start with the Answer

Yes, we're giving you the answer! Well, we're giving you the sum or the difference. Each number on the left is the sum or the difference of two numbers on the right. Draw lines from each sum or difference to their matching numbers. Go ahead, start with the answer!

Great going!
You found the answer, uh, I mean, the question. Now look around for the puzzle piece. Cut it out and drop it into the puzzle frame on page 64. Then tape or glue it in place.

Sums
1. 1.97
2. 3.477
3. 9.852
4. 5.221

1.32
2.45
3.14
0.65
1.027
1.432
6.712
3.789

0.567
7.643
1.027
0.235
1.321
1.25
0.962
6.372

Differences
5. 6.322
6. 0.727
7. 0.683
8. 5.345

22

NAME_____

Rock Climbing

Grab your boots and your rope, and scoop up some trail mix, too. You're about to go rock climbing. Start at the bottom of each pile. Multiply two numbers that are side by side. Then write the product on the rock above. Round each product to the nearest thousandth. Keep multiplying and writing the products until you've made it to the top.

> Where do you put the decimal point in the product? Count the number of places to the right of the decimal in the two factors. Then count over that many places in the product.
> .2 x .06 = .012

1.

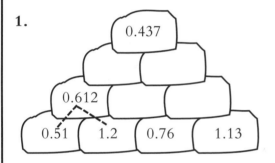

0.437

0.612

0.51 · 1.2 · 0.76 · 1.13

2.

1.112

1.32 · 1.06 · 0.75 · 1.27

3.

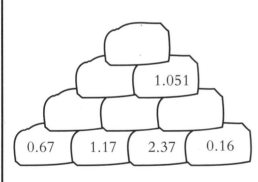

1.051

0.67 · 1.17 · 2.37 · 0.16

4.

0.269

2.07 · 2.01 · 0.35

NAME _____

Haunted Mansions

Gregor is looking for a certain haunted mansion. He was told to look for the one with 63.6 percent of its windows darkened. Help Gregor and find the percent of the darkened windows in each mansion. Then circle the mansion Gregor is looking for.

To write a fraction as a percent, change the fraction to a decimal and multiply by 100.

1. $\frac{3}{8}$ = 37.5% darkened

2. _____ % darkened

3. _____ % darkened

4. _____ % darkened

5. _____ % darkened

6. _____ % darkened

NAME_____

Mark It Down!

Are you ready for some bargains? Marjorie is—she works in a sporting goods store. She needs to mark down some prices for a big sale. Give Marjorie a hand, and figure out the price of each item when it is marked down. Write the marked down price next to the word *Now*.

Here's an example:
Was $10.00.
Marked down 20%.
$10 x .20 = $2.
$10 − $2 = $8.
Now $8.00

Great prices!
Now find the puzzle piece on this page and cut it out. Find its spot on the puzzle frame on page 64 and tape or glue it in place.

1. Was $29.95
Marked down 25%

Now _____

2. Was $15.75
Marked down 33%

Now _____

3. Was $75.98
Marked down 15%

Now _____

4. Was $52.35
Marked down 20%

Now _____

5. Was $129.49
Marked down 45%

Now _____

6. Was $99.95
Marked down 18%

Now _____

Grade 5

25

NAME _____

Hidden Moths

Calling all entomologists! That's you, by the way. An entomologist studies insects and stuff like that. So, where are the bugs on this page? They are camouflaged in the pictures. Instead of a magnifying glass, all you have to do to see the 8 hidden moths is shade the sections that have ratios equal to $\frac{2}{3}$. One is done for you.

If two fractions are equivalent, the ratios are equal.
If the cross products are equal, the fractions are equivalent.

$$\frac{2}{3} \times\!\!\!\times \frac{4}{6}$$

$\frac{5}{9}$ $\frac{20}{27}$ $\frac{12}{18}$ $\frac{9}{15}$

$\frac{6}{9}$ $\frac{4}{10}$ $\frac{12}{30}$

$\frac{30}{45}$

$\frac{16}{45}$ $\frac{25}{35}$ $\frac{15}{21}$

$\frac{15}{18}$ $\frac{35}{45}$ $\frac{26}{65}$

$\frac{36}{54}$ $\frac{9}{12}$ $\frac{17}{24}$

$\frac{5}{20}$ $\frac{38}{54}$

$\frac{18}{27}$ $\frac{10}{15}$

$\frac{3}{6}$ $\frac{42}{66}$

$\frac{18}{45}$ $\frac{4}{9}$ $\frac{15}{90}$

$\frac{24}{36}$ $\frac{21}{32}$ $\frac{44}{66}$ $\frac{7}{20}$

$\frac{2}{15}$

Dinosaur Shadows

Find out how big each dinosaur is. Figure out a proportion, as shown in the first problem. Then write the dinosaur's height on the line.

---

1. Brachiosaurus

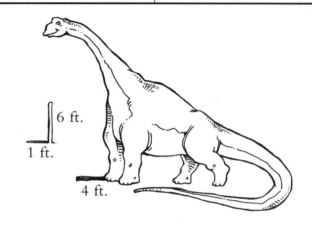

step 1: set up proportion

$$\frac{1 \text{ ft. (stake shadow)}}{6 \text{ ft. (stake)}} = \frac{4 \text{ ft. (dino shadow)}}{X \text{ ft. (dino)}}$$

step 2: cross multiply $1 \times X = 4 \times 6$

step 3: solve for X $X = 24$

6 ft.

1 ft.

4 ft.

Height: 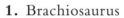 24 ft.

2. Tyrannosaurus

16 ft.

8 ft.

10 ft.

Height: _____

3. Duckbill

3 ft.

6 ft.

36 ft.

Height: _____

NAME _____

Tennis Ball Bounces

When a new tennis ball is dropped from a height of about 80 inches, it bounces several times. You can find the height of each bounce by multiplying the height of the previous bounce by 0.6. Use the data to complete the table below.

	first bounce	second bounce
example:	80 X 0.6 = 48	48 X 0.6 = 28.8

Complete the table to discover the height of the first ten bounces. Round to the nearest tenths of an inch. Then use the data to make a line graph of tennis ball bounces.

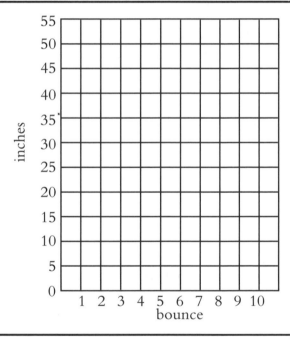

Bounce	Height (in.)
1	48
2	28.8
3	17.3
4	10.4
5	6.2
6	
7	
8	
9	
10	

Check Yourself: Work with a partner to actually do the bouncing. Stand on a sturdy chair or stepstool, and drop a tennis ball from about 80 inches (that's 6 feet, 8 inches). Have your partner catch the ball at the top of the bounce and then use a tape measure to check the height. Have your partner drop the ball from the height at which he caught it and measure the height again. Repeat 8 more times. How closely do your numbers match?

NAME_____

Graphing My Day

What do you do all day? How long do you do it? Find out. Make a list in the chart of what you do in a 24-hour period and about how long you spend doing it. Then follow the directions to complete the circle graph below.

Activity	Hours

Use the information in your chart to complete this circle graph. The circle graph is divided into 24 sections, one for each hour of the day. Label one section with the name of the activity for each hour you spend doing it. Then answer the questions below.

A Day in My Life

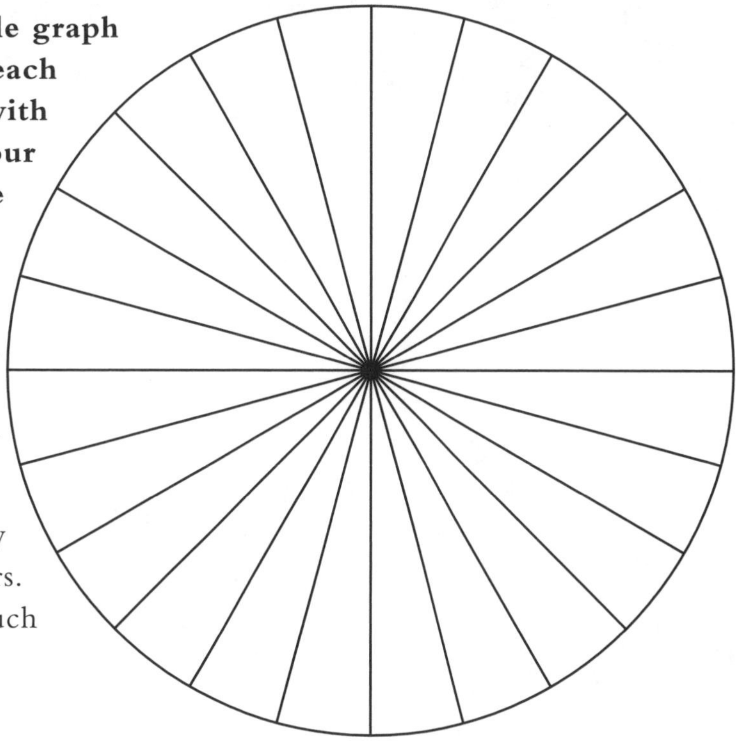

1. Which activity do you spend the most time doing?_____
2. Which activity do you spend the least time doing?_____

Around the House: Ask your family members to make circle graphs like yours. How do they spend their time? How much time do they waste?

NAME _____

Toss and Guess

Have you ever tossed the dice in a game and wondered what the chances were for a certain combination to come up? Now is your chance to find out. On the pairs of dice below, draw the correct number of dots to show all possible outcomes. Then use the dice to answer the questions below. One is done for you.

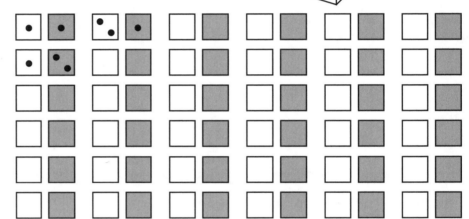

Now you know the toss of the dice! Cut out the puzzle piece. Pop it into the correct spot.

1. How many outcomes have a total of 7? ___6___

   What is the probability of getting 7?
   ___6___ out of 36
   or ___1___ out of ___6___

2. How many outcomes have a total of 5? _____

   What is the probability of getting 5?
   _____ out of 36
   or _____ out of _____

3. How many outcomes result in doubles? _____

   What is the probability of getting a double?
   _____ out of 36
   or _____ out of _____

4. How many outcomes result in double 1s? _____

   What is the probability of getting a double 1?
   _____ out of 36
   or _____ out of _____

30

NAME_____

Riddles and Puzzles

When you solve these riddles, you'll ride tall in the saddle!
And if you don't have a horse, at least you can hold your
head up high, right? Especially when you use logical
reasoning to solve these problems. Read each problem and
write the answer. Good luck, partner!

1.
Kim, Joan, Sally, and Tanya are each
wearing a different color bandanna.
The colors are blue, green, yellow,
and red. Neither Joan nor Sally likes
yellow. Kim was going to wear red,
but chose blue instead. Sally does
not have any green clothes. What
color is each cowgirl wearing?

_____

2. Two fathers and two sons divided 3
cactus pears among themselves. Each
person received 1 whole cactus pear.
How could this possibly be?

_____

3.
At the beginning of the summer on the
ranch, there was 1 water lily on the lake.
The area of the lake covered by water
lilies doubled every day. By the last
day in August, the lake was completely
covered. On what date was half of the
lake covered with water lilies?

_____

4. I'm a four-digit number. My ones
digit is the sum of my tens and
thousands digit. My tens digit is
one more than my thousands
digit. My hundreds digit is 1 less
than my ones digit. My thousands
digit is 3. What number am I?

_____

5. The fraction $\frac{2}{3}$ has an equivalent
fraction for which the sum of its
numerator and denominator is 30.
What is the equivalent fraction?

_____

6. Crazy Crackers had a special offer:
Collect 8 labels and get 1 bag free.
Lou persuaded all of his friends to
give him their labels. He collected
71 labels in all. How many free bags
of Crazy Crackers was Lou able
to get all together?_____

NAME _____

Magic Squares

A magician never tells the secret to the magic. But here's the secret to the magic number in Magic Squares: It's in the sums! The sum of the numbers in each row, column, and diagonal is the same. You can find the value for x or y in one of the puzzle squares. Then find the value of the other missing numbers. Add the numbers going across, down, and diagonally to find each magic number. Write it on the line. Abracadabra and away you go!

$x + 1$	$x - 6$	$x - 1$
$x - 4$	$x - 2$	$x = 17$
$x - 3$	$x + 2$	$x - 5$

Magic Number:

_____

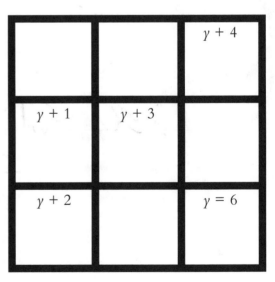

> Look in the squares to find out what number the letter represents. Then substitute the number for the letter in each expression.

Magic Number:

_____

		$y + 4$
$y + 1$	$y + 3$	
$y + 2$		$y = 6$

32

NAME_____

Really Big Numbers

What's the biggest number you can think of? Is it a million?
a billion? a trillion? Numbers go on forever, of course, and
there are some strange-sounding names for some really big
numbers. Take a *googol,* for example. It's a 1 followed by 100
zeros. Here's the start of a googol. Try finishing it.

$$1 \quad 0 \quad 0 \quad 0 \quad 0 \quad 0 \quad 0 \quad 0 \quad 0 \quad 0$$

_____

_____

Here are some really big facts, but not nearly as big as a googol. Match each
number with a fact. Write the number on the line to complete each one.

1. Your heart beats about_____ times a day.

2. The temperature at the center of the sun is about

 _____ ° F.

3. The sun is about _____ miles from Earth.

4. About _27,000,000_ people live in the United States.

5. Each day, about _____ of your body's cells

 are replaced.

6. Earth is about _____ years old.

7. About _5,770,000,000_ people live in the world.

8. There are about _____ stars.

27,000,000

200,000,000,000,000,000,000

250,000,000

93,000,000

100,000

4,500,000,000

5,770,000,000

2,000,000,000

Check Yourself: If you completed each fact correctly, the
numbers you used should be in order from least to greatest.

Around the House: Find some big number facts of your own.
Try looking in almanacs and encyclopedias. Use the facts to
impress your friends.

NAME _____

Did You Know?

Do you know these fun science facts? If you don't, don't worry. Add or subtract the numbers below. Write the sum or difference on the line. Then you'll complete each fact.

1.
$$\begin{array}{r} 13,279 \\ -\ 12,789 \\ \hline \end{array}$$

Did you know that there is enough salt in the oceans to cover all of the land in a layer _____ feet thick?

2.
$$\begin{array}{r} 41,892 \\ -\ 20,778 \\ \hline \end{array}$$

Did you know that a tiny insect called Forcipomyia can beat its wings _____ times per minute?

3.
$$\begin{array}{r} 12,345 \\ +\ 9,655 \\ \hline \end{array}$$

Did you know that the Arctic tern migrates more than_____ miles every year?

4.
$$\begin{array}{r} 1,258,632 \\ -\ 458,632 \\ \hline \end{array}$$

Did you know that there are over _____ different kinds of insects in the world?

5.
$$\begin{array}{r} 101,538 \\ +\ 198,462 \\ \hline \end{array}$$

Did you know that the blue whale, the largest living animal, can weigh as much as _____ pounds?

6.
$$\begin{array}{r} 79,843 \\ -\ 65,343 \\ \hline \end{array}$$

Did you know that the deepest ice in Antarctica is over _____ feet thick?

7.
$$\begin{array}{r} 296,435 \\ -\ 260,275 \\ \hline \end{array}$$

Did you know that the deepest place in the ocean is _____ feet below sea level in the Marianas Trench?

8.
$$\begin{array}{r} 220,214 \\ +\ 129,786 \\ \hline \end{array}$$

Did you know that there are more than _____ different kinds of plants in the world?

NAME_____

Crossnumber Puzzle

Look sharp! This is not just another crossword puzzle. In fact, it's not a crossword puzzle at all. It's a crossnumber puzzle. Read each problem. Then multiply or divide to get the answer. Write the answer where it belongs in the crossnumber puzzle.

Across

  1. 780 X 127
  3. 4,032 ÷ 72
  4. 8,025 ÷ 25
  6. 128 X 334
  8. 8,990 ÷ 31
  9. 563 X 317
12. 929 X 4
14. 1,015 X 42
16. 12,051 ÷ 13
18. 5,535 ÷ 123
19. 2,226 ÷ 6
20. 2,990 ÷ 65

Down

  1. 5,472 ÷ 6
  2. 31,127 X 2
  3. 6,228 ÷ 12
  5. 7,200 ÷ 30
  7. 969 X 74
  8. 3,851 X 6
10. 1,927 X 12
11. 528 X 57
13. 5,289 ÷ 41
15. 383 X 7
17. 2,409 ÷ 33

Try working Across first. Then you'll have some hints about the Down clues.

Cut out the puzzle piece below. Put it where it belongs.

NAME _____

Positively Puzzling

Don't be so negative . . . unless it helps you complete these puzzles. Read the sentences. Add the integers to solve the puzzles. Now, it's OK to be negative, or positive, or both if that will plug the holes in the puzzle. Good luck!

Remember when you add integers:
positive + positive = positive
negative + negative = negative
positive + negative = positive or negative, depending on the sign of the largest addend.

You can add 3 integers by first adding any 2 and then adding the sum and the third integer.

1. Write the integers −1, +1, +2, and +3 in the empty circles so the sum along each side is +1.

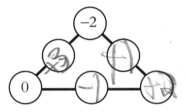

2. Write the integers −2, −1, 0, +1, and +2 in the empty circles so the sum along each spoke through the center is −5.

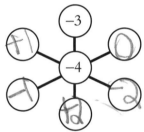

3. Write the integers −3, −2, −1, 0, +1, +2, in the empty boxes so the sum along each row, column, and diagonal is −3.

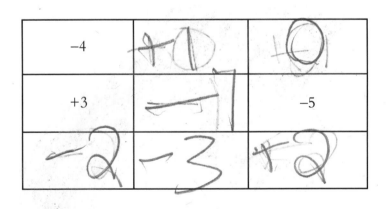

−4	+1	+1
+3	−1	−5
−2	−3	+2

NAME_____

Stay on the Path

If you can't follow the yellow brick road, try following the path around these traceables. Trace the entire figure without lifting your pencil. You can't retrace any lines, but you can cross over them. Then write down the number of squares and triangles you found along the way.

1. number of squares _____ 1
   number of triangles _____ 1

2. number of squares _____ 1
   number of triangles _____ 5

3. number of squares _____ 9
   number of triangles _____ 5

4. number of squares _____ 3
   number of triangles _____ 2

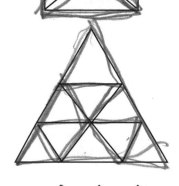

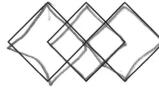

Don't forget to cut out the puzzle piece and put it in the frame on page 64.

Around the House: Test someone at home. How quickly can the person follow the paths?

Grade 6

37

NAME _____

Make It Fit

Can you use a compass and a ruler to draw a triangle in a circle? Follow the directions, and you'll do it. You can draw any triangle in a circle so the circle touches each point, or vertex, of the triangle.

A *perpendicular bisector* is a line that crosses another line and is perpendicular to it. That means it forms right angles at the crossing point.

1. Open your compass wider than half of *AB*.

2. Place the point of your compass on *A*. Draw an arc above and below *AB*. Keep the compass opening the same and repeat with your compass point on *B*.

3. Draw a line between the points of intersection of the arcs.

4. Repeat for *AC* and *CB*. Then extend the perpendicular bisectors until they meet at a point inside the triangle.

5. Use the point where the perpendicular bisectors meet at the center to draw a circle that touches each vertex of the triangle.

Use this triangle. Draw a circle so it touches each vertex.

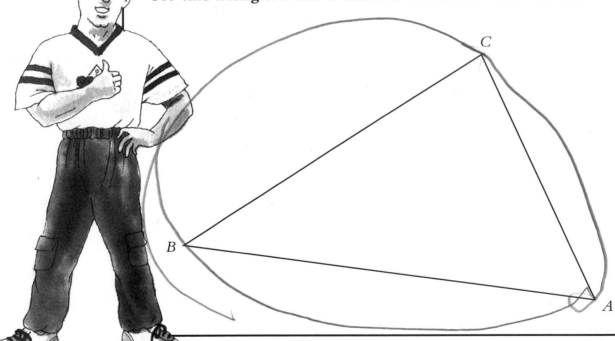

NAME_____

Snip, Snip, Snip

You have incredible power in your hands! As long as you're holding those little scissors, anyway. With one cut, you can change these polygons into other polygons. Find a pair of scissors and then follow along and get ready to snip, snip, snip. Here's what you do:

1. Look at each larger shape and then the smaller shape inside. Carefully trace the larger shape onto another piece of paper. Then cut it out.

2. Now think! Where will you cut the larger shape so you can put the two pieces together to make the smaller shape? (It needs to be the same shape, not the same size.) Check it out by drawing a line in the figure on this page.

3. Ready? Go ahead and cut. Now put your pieces together and ta-da-a-a—a new polygon!

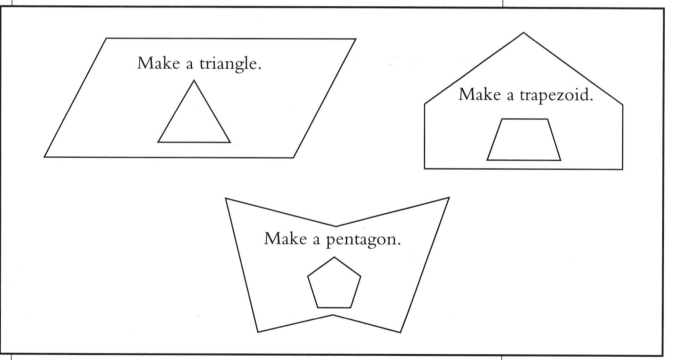

Around the House: Try these out on someone at home. Give them a little coaching to help out.

NAME _____

Pentamino Combos

A pentamino is a little like a domino. But where a domino is made of two squares, a pentamino is made of five squares. (*Penta* means five.) To be a pentamino, each of the five squares in a figure has to have one whole side touching the whole side of another square. Look at the figures below. Put an X on those that are not pentaminos. Then follow the directions below.

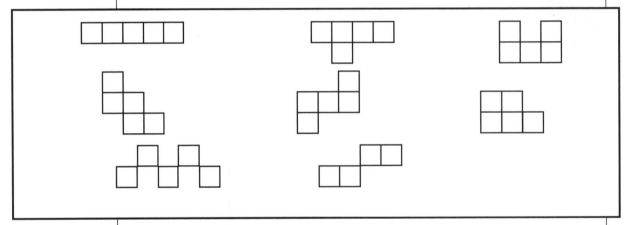

1. It's possible to make six more pentaminos that are different from the ones above. Use the graph grid at the bottom of the page to draw as many of the other six as you can.

2. Eight pentaminos, including some of the ones you drew, can be folded up to form open "cartons." See if you can figure out which ones they are. **Hint:** First trace your pentaminos. Then cut them out.

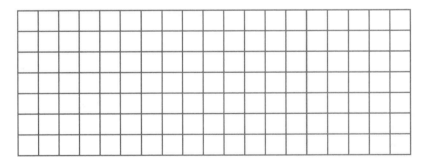

NAME_____

What's the Shape?

Wait a minute, aren't these pentaminos? Look again—there are six congruent squares in these figures. Think, now, what three-dimensional figure would you get if you folded them up? All right, go ahead and fold them. Trace the figures, cut them out, and fold them up.

Write down the name of the three dimensional figure.

Congruent means the same shape and size.

Great folding!
Now cut out the puzzle piece and drop it into the puzzle frame on page 64. Then glue or tape it in place.

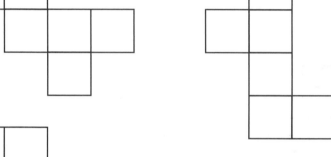

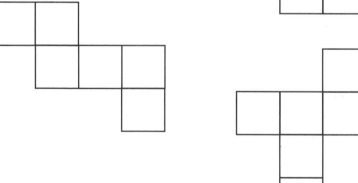

Around the House: There are seven more patterns that make this same shape. How many can you figure out? Draw your patterns on graph paper, cut them out, and fold them up.

NAME _____

Make an Octahedron

Are octahedrons dangerous? Can their tentacles grab you and . . . Oh, sorry, we mean the eight-sided space figure, not the eight-armed sea animal. Here's an octahedron to look at. See, it's not dangerous at all.

Octahedron

Here's a pattern for making an octahedron. Just trace it on another sheet of paper, cut it out, fold it up, and tape the edges together. Then try the activity below.

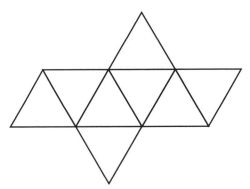

A *regular octahedron* is made up of 8 equilateral triangles.

Here are four other patterns for making an octahedron. Six more are possible. See if you can draw some on a separate sheet of paper.

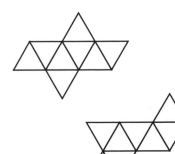

NAME

Point of View

You've folded, you've taped, you've looked at shapes from all different angles. Now use your imagination. Suppose each of these flattened-out cubes is all taped together and sitting on your desk. Which one would you actually be looking at? Circle your choice.

1.

    a. b. c. d.

2.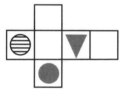

    a. b. c. d.

3.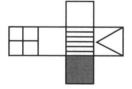

    a. b. c. d.

4.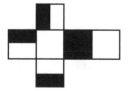

    a. b. c. d.

> **Nice work!**
> You have a great
> point of view.

NAME _____

Sorting Boxes

As long as you're cleaning out the basement, you might as well sort these boxes. First find the volume of each box and write it on the line. Next list the boxes in order from least volume to greatest volume. Then answer the questions.

A.

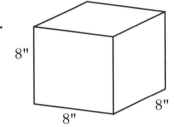

Volume _____

B.

Volume _____

> The volume of a rectangular prism is length x width x height.

C.

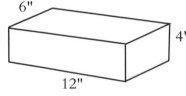

Volume _____

D.

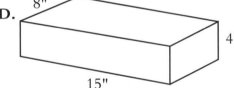

Volume _____

Box order: _____

1. The height of this box is half its width.

Box _____

2. This box is two feet long.

Box _____

3. The length and height of this box are the same.

Box _____

4. The length of this box is twice its width.

Box _____

Circles Within Circles

Do you feel like you're going around in circles?
Well, straighten out and solve this puzzle. What's the total
area of the shaded parts and the total area of the unshaded
part in the figure below? All the information you need is
right here once you answer the questions.
Use another sheet of paper if you need to. Write the
answers on the lines.

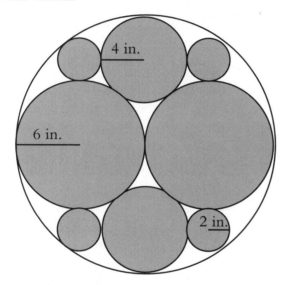

The formula
for finding the area
of a circle is
$A = \pi \times (radius)^2$.
Or,
$A = \pi \times radius \times radius$.
Remember $\pi = 3.14$

It's time to cut out
the puzzle piece.
Glue or tape it in
place on page 64.

1. What is the total area of the four small circles? (Hint: Find the area
    of one small circle. Then times it by 4.) _____

2. What is the total area of the two medium circles? _____

3. What is the total area of the two large circles? _____

4. What is the total area of the large outer circle? (Hint: The diameter
    of the large circle equals the radius of the outer circle.) _____

**Now you have all the information you need to answer these
two questions.**

5. What is the total area of the shaded part inside the circle? _____

6. What is the total area of the unshaded part inside the circle? _____

Grade 6   **45**

NAME _____

Lunar Landing

"We have touchdown!" On July 20, 1969, an American astronaut climbed out of the Apollo 11 lunar module and became the first person to set foot on the moon. Who was that person? Find the sums and differences of these mixed number problems. Circle the correct answer to each problem. Then write its letter above the matching problem number at the bottom of the page. When you finish, you will have spelled out the name of that lucky astronaut.

To add or subtract mixed fractions, first add the fractions. Then add the whole numbers. Reduce the fractions if possible. Don't forget to make sure you are working with common denominators.

1. $3\frac{1}{2} + 5\frac{1}{4}$	**R** $8\frac{3}{4}$	**O** $9\frac{3}{4}$	**G** $7\frac{3}{4}$
2. $4\frac{7}{8} + 3\frac{1}{3}$	**S** $7\frac{5}{24}$	**E** $8\frac{1}{6}$	**A** $8\frac{5}{24}$
3. $6\frac{3}{4} - 5\frac{5}{12}$	**B** $1\frac{5}{12}$	**M** $2\frac{5}{12}$	**G** $1\frac{1}{3}$
4. $12\frac{4}{5} - 7\frac{3}{4}$	**I** $4\frac{3}{10}$	**L** $5\frac{1}{20}$	**C** $6\frac{3}{10}$
5. $6\frac{1}{4} - 1\frac{1}{2}$	**D** $5\frac{3}{4}$	**F** $3\frac{3}{4}$	**O** $4\frac{3}{4}$
6. $2\frac{1}{2} + 4\frac{3}{4}$	**H** $8\frac{1}{4}$	**M** $7\frac{1}{4}$	**K** $8\frac{1}{4}$
7. $7\frac{3}{4} - 5\frac{1}{4}$	**P** $1\frac{1}{4}$	**R** $3\frac{1}{4}$	**T** $2\frac{1}{2}$
8. $9 - 3\frac{3}{4}$	**E** $5\frac{1}{4}$	**S** $4\frac{3}{4}$	**U** $6\frac{3}{4}$
9. $2\frac{3}{8} + 4\frac{3}{4}$	**N** $7\frac{1}{8}$	**Y** $8\frac{1}{8}$	**A** $6\frac{1}{8}$
10. $3\frac{5}{6} + 8\frac{3}{4}$	**E** $11\frac{1}{3}$	**L** $13\frac{1}{3}$	**N** $12\frac{7}{12}$
11. $7\frac{1}{4} - 6\frac{5}{6}$	**O** $\frac{1}{3}$	**S** $\frac{5}{12}$	**F** $\frac{1}{2}$
12. $6\frac{7}{10} + 11\frac{3}{10}$	**D** 17	**T** 19	**R** 18
13. $14\frac{3}{4} - 5$	**I** $9\frac{3}{4}$	**P** $8\frac{3}{4}$	**B** $10\frac{3}{4}$

$\overline{9}$ $\overline{8}$ $\overline{13}$ $\overline{4}$ $\overline{2}$ $\overline{1}$ $\overline{6}$ $\overline{11}$ $\overline{7}$ $\overline{12}$ $\overline{5}$ $\overline{10}$ $\overline{3}$

Make a Fraction

Making a fraction is not quite like making a cake, but we are giving you the ingredients. For each problem, use two of the three digits in the boxes to cook up a fraction that completes the equation. Write the fraction in the box. The first one is done for you.

1. ☐1 ☐2 ☐3

$$\frac{1}{4} \div \frac{\boxed{2}}{\boxed{3}} = \frac{3}{8}$$

2. ☐3 ☐4 ☐5

$$3 \div \frac{\boxed{}}{\boxed{}} = 5$$

3. ☐5 ☐6 ☐8

$$\frac{5}{8} \div \frac{\boxed{}}{\boxed{}} = 1$$

4. ☐4 ☐5 ☐6

$$\frac{3}{4} \div \frac{\boxed{}}{\boxed{}} = \frac{9}{10}$$

5. ☐1 ☐2 ☐4

$$\frac{5}{7} \div \frac{\boxed{}}{\boxed{}} = 1\frac{3}{7}$$

6. ☐2 ☐3 ☐4

$$\frac{5}{8} \div \frac{\boxed{}}{\boxed{}} = \frac{15}{16}$$

7. ☐4 ☐5 ☐8

$$\frac{1}{2} \div \frac{\boxed{}}{\boxed{}} = \frac{4}{5}$$

8. ☐1 ☐2 ☐3

$$3 \div \frac{\boxed{}}{\boxed{}} = 4\frac{1}{2}$$

Remember when you divide fractions, you invert the dividend and multiply. Reduce them if possible.

NAME _____

Fractured Facts

Here's a game to play with fractions. First, read each question and guess the answer. Then do the division and circle the correct quotient. That'll show you the answer to the question.

> When you divide mixed numbers write the mixed numbers as improper fractions. Then divide as you would any other fractions.

1. $3\frac{2}{3} \div 5\frac{1}{2} =$ What is the average distance from Mars to Earth?

$16\frac{2}{3}$ about 1,000,000 miles

$1\frac{1}{3}$ about 49,000,000,000 miles

$\frac{2}{3}$ about 49,000,000 miles

2. $2\frac{3}{4} \div \frac{1}{2} =$ About how much gold is stored in Fort Knox?

$3\frac{1}{2}$ about $6 million worth

$5\frac{1}{2}$ about $6 billion worth

$3\frac{1}{4}$ about $60 billion worth

3. $2\frac{3}{5} \div 1\frac{5}{8} =$ How long is the Mississippi River?

$\frac{3}{5}$ 5,283 miles

$1\frac{3}{5}$ 2,348 miles

$3\frac{3}{5}$ 1,348 miles

4. $4\frac{1}{8} \div 1\frac{4}{7} =$ The Cullinan diamond is the largest diamond ever found. How much does it weigh?

$2\frac{5}{8}$ 3,106 carats

$2\frac{5}{16}$ 1,306 carats

$4\frac{5}{8}$ 506 carats

5. $3\frac{3}{4} \div 1\frac{2}{3} =$ How old was Neil Armstrong when he landed on the moon?

$2\frac{1}{8}$ 28 years old

$3\frac{1}{4}$ 32 years old

$2\frac{1}{4}$ 38 years old

6. $7\frac{1}{2} \div 1\frac{1}{4} =$ The bee hummingbird is the smallest bird. About how much does it weigh?

7 $\frac{1}{10}$ of a pound

$7\frac{1}{8}$ 1 ounce

6 $\frac{1}{10}$ of an ounce

48

NAME _____

Find the Location

You like to be in the right place at the right time, don't you? Being in the right place is pretty important for decimals, too. Look at the decimals. Then use the clues to locate the correct decimal for each item. Circle the decimal.

1.

- Each digit is an even number.
- The digit in the hundredths place is 4.
- The digit in the tenths place is 1 less than 7.

2.

- Rounded to the nearest ten, the number is 20.
- The sum of the digits is 16.
- The digit in the tenths place is greater than the digit in the hundredths place.

3.

- The digit in the tenths place is 5.
- Each digit is different.
- The digit in the hundredths place is 8.
- The digit in the hundredths place is twice the digit in the ones place.

4.

- Each digit is an odd number.
- The digit in the hundredths place is 1.
- The digit in the tenths place is 7.

5.

- The number is greater than 30.
- The digit in the tens place is 1 less than the digit in the tenths place.
- The digit in the ones place is 1 less than the digit in the tenths place.

6.

- Each digit is different.
- The digit in the thousandths place is 1 more than the digit in the ones place.
- The digit in the hundredths place is 2 more than the digit in the thousandths place.

Grade 6

49

NAME _____

Pick-a-Pattern

To change a fraction to a decimal, divide the numerator by the denominator. You can show a repeating decimal by drawing a line over the repeating part: $\frac{1}{11}$ = 0.$\overline{09}$.

Cut out the puzzle piece. Put it in place on page 64.

Some patterns repeat the same colors over and over again. The patterns below have decimals that repeat, and repeat again. Turn the fractions into repeating decimals. Write the repeating decimal on the line. Then, look for the pattern. Write it down, too. (You'll probably want to use a calculator.)

1. $\frac{1}{9}$ = ___.1___ $\frac{2}{9}$ = ___2___ $\frac{3}{9}$ = ___.3___

   $\frac{4}{9}$ = _____ $\frac{5}{9}$ = _____ $\frac{6}{9}$ = _____

What's the pattern? _____

_____

2. $\frac{1}{11}$ = ___.$\overline{09}$___ $\frac{2}{11}$ = _____ $\frac{3}{11}$ = _____

   $\frac{4}{11}$ = _____ $\frac{5}{11}$ = _____ $\frac{6}{11}$ = _____

What's the pattern? _____

_____

3. $\frac{1}{33}$ = _____ $\frac{2}{33}$ = _____ $\frac{3}{33}$ = _____

   $\frac{4}{33}$ = _____ $\frac{5}{33}$ = _____ $\frac{6}{33}$ = _____

What's the pattern? _____

_____

4. $\frac{1}{99}$ = _____ $\frac{2}{99}$ = _____ $\frac{3}{99}$ = _____

   $\frac{4}{99}$ = _____ $\frac{5}{99}$ = _____ $\frac{6}{99}$ = _____

What's the pattern? _____

_____

NAME_____

The Product Is . . . ?

Don't be fooled! These look like multiplication problems, but they're not. In order to find the missing factors you need to—divide! Divide the product by the factor given for each problem (a–f). Then write the correct factor from the box on the line. Remember, the factors in each problem must equal the product that is given. The first one is done for you.

1. The product is 4.32. | Factors: 2, 4, 5, 6, 8, 9 |

   a. 2.16 X __2__   **b.** 0.864 X _____   **c.** 0.72 X _____

   d. 1.08 X _____   **e.** 0.48 X _____   **f.** 0.54 X _____

2. The product is 1.26. | Factors: 2, 3, 4, 5, 7, 9 |

   a. 0.63 X _____   **b.** 0.252 X _____   **c.** 0.18 X _____

   d. 0.315 X _____ **e.** 0.14 X _____   **f.** 0.42 X _____

3. The product is 2.16. | Factors: 2, 4, 5, 6, 8, 9 |

   a. 0.27 X _____   **b.** 0.54 X _____   **c.** 0.24 X _____

   d. 1.08 X _____   **e.** 0.36 X _____   **f.** 0.432 X _____

When dividing decimals, move the decimal point in the divisor to the right to make a whole number. Move the decimal point in the dividend the same number of places to the right. Then divide.

Check Yourself: Remember that you can check your division results by multiplying.

NAME _____

Make One

In order to make exactly one, you have to use three.
Find the three numbers in each group that, when added
together, equal 1. Use a pencil to shade in the 3 tokens you
can use to "Make One." The first one is done for you.

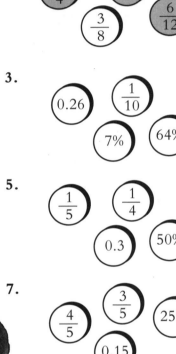

1.

2.

3.

4.

5.

6.

7.

8.

9.

10.

Here's a tip:
You might want to
change each
number to the
same form. Make
them all fractions,
decimals, or
percents.

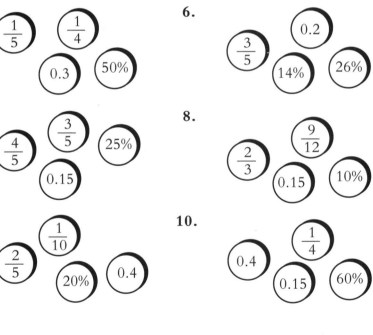

Around the House: Set a time limit and see how quickly your
friends and family can choose three to "Make One."

52

Grade 6

NAME _____

Percent Puzzle

Here's a puzzle you won't find in your daily newspaper. Put aside your dictionary, and call up your percent know-how. Figure out the answers to the problems. Then, write them where they belong in the puzzle.

Across

1. $\frac{1}{4}$ is ___ %
2. $\frac{1}{3}$ is about ___ %
4. 40% of 50
5. $\frac{3}{4}$ is ___%
7. 0.61 is ___ %
9. 80% of 50
10. 3 less than $\frac{3}{4}$ is ___ %
11. the sum of this number plus "1 across" is the percent that equals $\frac{12}{25}$

12. 50% of 50% of 112
13. about 15% of 233
14. 10% of 620
15. this % of 100 is 7 less than a quarter
16. the nearest whole number % for $\frac{2}{9}$
17. this percent is the same as $\frac{164}{328}$
18. $\frac{1}{2}$ of $\frac{1}{2}$ is ___%
20. this percent is 58% less than 100%
21. $\frac{1}{2}$ of $\frac{2}{5}$ is ___ %

22. $\frac{13}{50}$ is ___ %
23. 30% of 180
24. if you have this %, you have all but $\frac{1}{20}$ of it

> To change a fraction to a percent, change the fraction to a decimal and multiply by 100.

Down

1. the number of thousandths in 20%
3. $36\frac{1}{4}$ % in ten thousands
4. this percent is 76% less than 100%
5. $\frac{7}{9}$ is about ___ thousands
6. $\frac{13}{25}$ is ___%
8. an unlucky percent
12. 55% of 40

13. $\frac{3}{8}$ rounded to the nearest whole number percent
14. $62\frac{1}{4}$ % is this many ten thousandths
15. 35% of this number is 35
16. 30% of 80
17. this many hundredths equals 52%
18. $\frac{9}{4}$ is ___ %
19. 40% of 140 is ___

NAME _____

Letter Ratios

What are all of these words doing in a math activity? Relax.
You don't have to know what they mean, you just have to
look at the letters. Look at the words in each row. First,
find the ratio of vowels to the total number of letters in
each word. Then circle the two words in the row that have
the same ratio. Write the ratio on the lines. The first one is
done for you.

You are quite the
ratio reader! Now
find the puzzle
piece on this page.
Cut it out and
locate where it
belongs on the
puzzle frame on
page 64. Tape or
glue it in place.

1. (design) (fin) match   trouble   1 (vowel) to 3 (letters)

2. feature seem   alike   leak   _____ to _____

3. final   cooler wash   seek   _____ to _____

4. floor   fast   blast   slam   _____ to _____

5. knock   heroic different listen   _____ to _____

6. lodge   moose piano   emit   _____ to _____

7. badge   floor fossil   graph   _____ to _____

8. harvest hound lecture leather   _____ to _____

9. ground   maintain network magazine _____ to _____

10. neighborhood nutritious respectful intersection

_____ to _____

54

NAME

Create a Masterpiece

You can create a masterpiece! Just use what you know about scale to enlarge this picture of a unicorn. Draw what you see in each square of the smaller grid onto the corresponding square of the larger grid. Use crayons or markers to color your masterpiece. Then answer the question.

How many times larger is your drawing than the original? _____

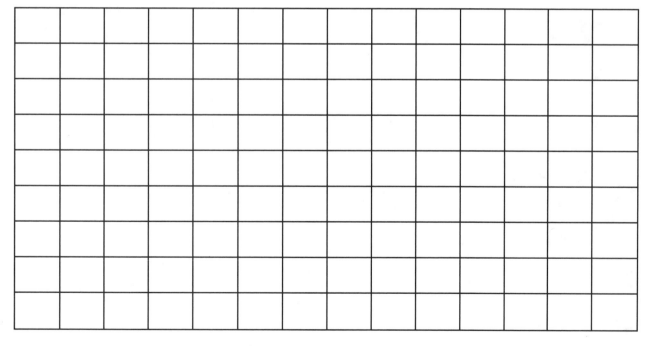

NAME _____

Get the Message

Can you discover the message written on the graph? Try this one. On the graph, plot each ordered pair of numbers. Then connect the points in the order shown by the arrows. Read the message. The first two points have been done.

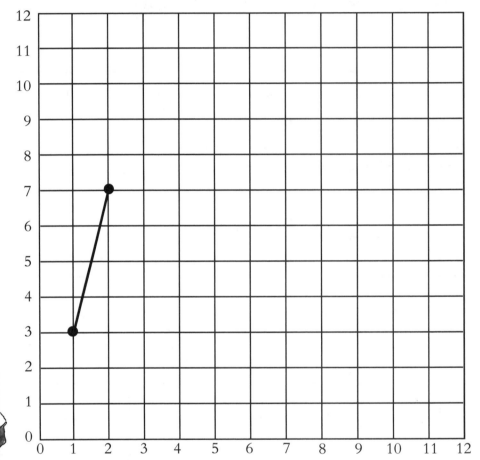

The first number in an ordered pair tells how many places you move across, or horizontally.

The second number tells how many places you move up, or vertically.

Ordered Pairs

(1,3) ⟶ (2,7) ⟶ (1,7) ⟶ (3,3) ⟶ (4,5) ⟶ (5,5) ⟶

(6,3) ⟶ (7,5) ⟶ (7,1) ⟶ (6,2) ⟶ (8,4) ⟶ (10,5) ⟶

(8,5) ⟶ (8,3) ⟶ (10,3)

NAME _____

Who's Faster?

Here are some activities to have some speedy fun with. You won't need a crash helmet, but you will need a partner (or pretend you're two people) and a clock with a second hand. Here's what you do:

1. One person performs each activity below, and the other person is the timekeeper. Write down the time it takes to do each activity.
2. Players switch roles and repeat. (Or, do it again, if you're on your own.)
3. Use the double bar graph to show and compare the times for each player.

Activities:

a. Say the alphabet.
b. Write the numbers from 1 to 50.
c. Say this tongue twister:
   Peter Piper picked a peck of pickled peppers;
   A peck of pickled peppers Peter Piper picked.
   If Peter Piper picked a peck of pickled peppers,
   Where's the peck of pickled peppers Peter Piper picked?

Choose a reasonable scale for your graph. Assign a different color or shading for each player.

Wow! You're faster than the speed of light—almost. Now, how quickly can you find where the puzzle piece belongs in the frame on page 64? Tape or glue it in place.

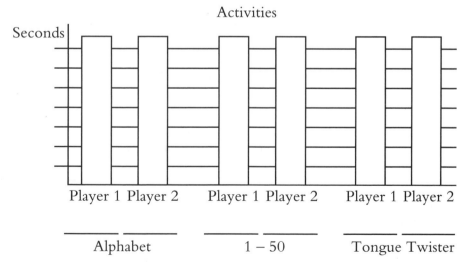

NAME _____

Spin a Win

To play this game, pretend you are spinning the spinner three times. If the sum of the spins were exactly 7, you would win! In the tables below, list all the possible outcomes of three spins of the spinner. Put a check next to each set of spins that equals 7. Then answer the question below.

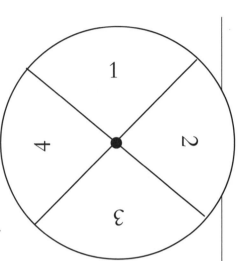

Spin 1	Spin 2	Spin 3
1	1	1
1	1	2
1	1	3
1	1	4
1	2	1
1	2	2

Spin 1	Spin 2	Spin 3
2	1	1

Spin 1	Spin 2	Spin 3
3	1	1

Spin 1	Spin 2	Spin 3
4	1	1

What are your chances, or the probability, of having spins that total 7?

_____ out of _____ chances of having three spins that total 7.

Probability
Use tree diagrams
to find probable outcomes

NAME _____

How Many Possibilities?

You are designing the *logo*, or symbol, for your nature club. The club members have narrowed the design down to either a triangle or an octagon shape with a bear, a bald eagle, or a dolphin on it. The most popular colors are green, blue, brown, and yellow. How many possibilities does that give you to work with? Complete the tree diagram to show them all. Then answer the questions.

Tree diagrams are a good way to figure out different combinations. Write the appropriate possibilities in the boxes. Then connect everything with lines.

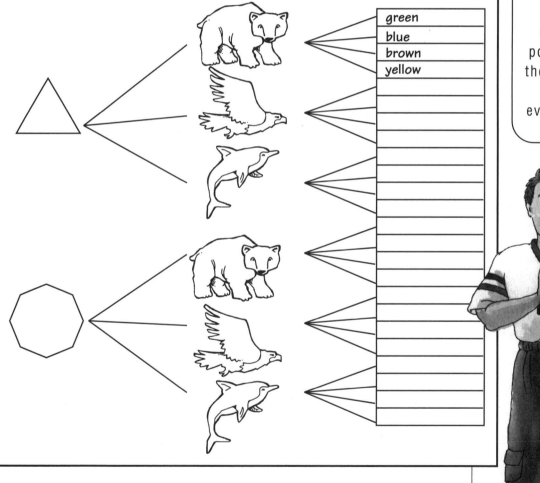

green
blue
brown
yellow

1. How many possible outcomes does the tree diagram show? _____

2. What's your favorite combination? _____

NAME _____

The Sieve of Eratosthenes

All right, *who* was Eratosthenes and *what* is a sieve? Well, Eratosthenes was a mathematician in ancient Greece who developed a way to find prime numbers. And a sieve is a strainer. So what does a strainer have to do with math? In Eratosthenes' method you "strain" out numbers until the only numbers left are prime numbers from 1 through 100. That's why it's called . . . The Sieve of Eratosthenes.

Give it a try by following the directions below.

1. Shade out 1.
2. Two is the first prime number. Now shade out all the even numbers except 2.
3. The second prime number is 3. Shade out all multiples of 3 except 3.
4. Five is the next prime number. Shade out all multiples of 5 except 5.

5. Seven is the next prime number. Shade out all multiples of 7 except 7. There will only be a few multiples of 7 that aren't already shaded.
6. You're finished at last. All the unshaded numbers on your chart are prime. You should have 25 of them.

A *prime number* is a whole number greater than one with exactly two factors. The factors are the number itself and 1.

1	2	3	4	5	6	7	8	9	10
11	12	13	14	15	16	17	18	19	20
21	22	23	24	25	26	27	28	29	30
31	32	33	34	35	36	37	38	39	40
41	42	43	44	45	46	47	48	49	50
51	52	53	54	55	56	57	58	59	60
61	62	63	64	65	66	67	68	69	70
71	72	73	74	75	76	77	78	79	80
81	82	83	84	85	86	87	88	89	90
91	92	93	94	95	96	97	98	99	100

NAME_____

Circle Puzzles

Are you seeing spots? Take it easy, they're not spots—they're circle puzzles. And the best way to solve them is "guess and check." Yep, you've got to give it your best guess, check your sum, and then give it another guess (if you have to). Of course, think carefully about your guesses before you put in the numbers. That way, you've got a pretty good shot at getting it right the first time!

1. Put the numbers 1, 2, 4, 5, 6, and 8 in the empty circles so that the sum of four circles in a row equals 26.

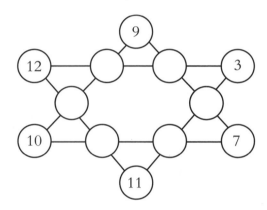

2. Put the numbers 1, 2, 3, 4, 5, 6, and 7 in the circles so the sum of four circles in a row equals 30.

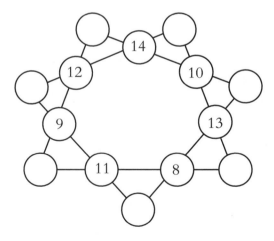

NAME _____

Picture Solvers

On this page a picture is worth the solution to each problem. After you read each problem, complete the picture in the space to find the solution.

1. A honey bee leaves its hive and flies to a flower 100 feet away. After each trip it returns to the hive and flies to a new flower half as far away as the one before. How far does the bee travel if the last flower it visits is 12.5 feet away?

_____

2. On his way to his job at the zoo, Marc passes Mike's Deli, Creature Comforts pet store, the post office, and the Read More bookstore. Mike's Deli is next to the zoo. The post office is between Read More and Mike's Deli. When Marc leaves home, he passes Creature Comforts first. In what order does he pass each place on his way to the zoo?

_____

3. Five children had a race to the bus stop. Rusty got there after Laura and Meg. Meg was first. Rusty was between Don and Laura. Betty was last. Which person finished in third place?

_____

NAME_____

Algebra Puzzle

Does this look familiar? You've done puzzles like this with words, and you've done a puzzle like this with percents. This one is different because you have to solve the equation to find the answer that goes in the puzzle itself. A calculator will be a handy thing to use for this little puzzler.

Across

1. $6x = 1{,}926$
3. $25y = 5{,}950$
5. $s \times 45 = 14{,}355$
6. $f - 50 = 58$
8. $41 = 3075/y$
9. $p + 316 = 736$
10. $n + 78.9 = 143.9$
13. $c - 467 = 352$
15. $5{,}263 - p = 4{,}707$
16. $5.12x = 506.88$
17. $3.2r = 1{,}974.4$

Down

2. $a \div 36 = 671$
3. $f \times 48 = 1{,}392$
4. $m + 546 = 1{,}411$
5. $162 + q = 512$
7. $c \times 43 = 3{,}612$
11. $617 + h = 1{,}206$
12. $d \div 4 = 41$
14. $149 = 14{,}304/z$
15. $73 \times y = 4{,}161$

Wow!
Now find the puzzle piece on this page and cut it out. Find its spot in the puzzle frame on page 64 and tape or glue it in place.

Puzzle

Here's where you glue or paste the puzzle pieces you cut out. When you put them all in place, you'll see your secret message.

64

Answers

Page 1

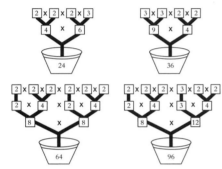

Page 2
1. 123,456,789
2. 987,654,321
3. 8,497
4. 35,124
5. 498,765
6. 613,425
7. 632,471
8. 123,456

Page 3

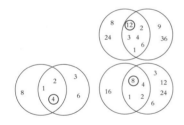

Page 4
Riddle:
A Cold

Page 5
2. 15 days   3. 24 days   4. 60 days

Page 6

132 x 265 = 34,980	426 x 265 = 112,890
132 x 597 = 78,804	426 x 597 = 254,322
132 x 709 = 93,588	426 x 709 = 302,034
132 x 815 = 107,580	426 x 815 = 347,190
350 x 265 = 92,750	649 x 265 = 171,985
350 x 597 = 208,950	649 x 597 = 387,453
350 x 709 = 248,150	649 x 709 = 460,141
350 x 815 = 285,250	649 x 815 = 528,935

Page 7

A. 125 R4   F. 79 R7
B. 91 R9   G. 96 R8
C. 24 R2   H. 21 R1
D. 12 R3   I. 86 R6
E. 52 R5

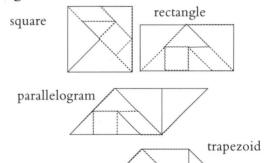

A. 4	B. 9	C. 2
D. 3	E. 5	F. 7
G. 8	H. 1	I. 6

Magic Number: 15

Page 8

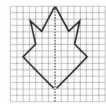

square

rectangle

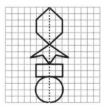

parallelogram

trapezoid

Page 9
Hexagon patterns should be different from each other.

Page 10
1. 27 triangles
2.

Page 11

Page 12
1. cylinder
2. rectangular prism
3. square pyramid

Page 13

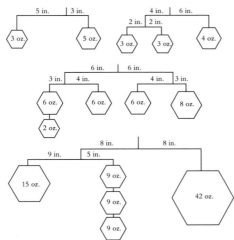

Page 14

1.
top	18 sq. in.
bottom	18 sq. in.
front side	12 sq. in.
back side	12 sq. in.
left side	6 sq. in.
right side	6 sq. in.
total area	72 sq. in.

2.
top	48 sq. in.
bottom	48 sq. in.
front side	36 sq. in.
back side	36 sq. in.
left side	12 sq. in.
right side	12 sq. in.
total area	192 sq. in.

Page 15

1. Argentina $\frac{11}{6}$ — $1\frac{5}{6}$ Buenos Aires
2. Bolivia $\frac{17}{8}$ — $2\frac{1}{8}$ La Paz
3. Brazil $\frac{7}{5}$ — $1\frac{2}{5}$ Brasilia
4. Chile $\frac{10}{4}$ — $2\frac{1}{2}$ Santiago
5. Colombia $\frac{21}{12}$ — $1\frac{3}{4}$ Bogotá
6. Ecuador $\frac{16}{9}$ — $1\frac{7}{9}$ Quito
7. Guyana $\frac{13}{5}$ — $2\frac{3}{5}$ Georgetown
8. Paraguay $\frac{18}{10}$ — $1\frac{4}{5}$ Asunción
9. Peru $\frac{21}{8}$ — $2\frac{5}{8}$ Lima
10. Suriname $\frac{12}{7}$ — $1\frac{5}{7}$ Paramaribo
11. Uruguay $\frac{24}{9}$ — $2\frac{2}{3}$ Montevideo
12. Venezuela $\frac{19}{2}$ — $9\frac{1}{2}$ Caracas

Page 16

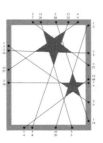

Page 17

A $= \frac{3}{4}$	N $= \frac{7}{32}$	W $= \frac{3}{10}$
B $= \frac{1}{2}$	O $= \frac{11}{14}$	X $= \frac{3}{20}$
C $= \frac{7}{10}$	P $= \frac{17}{32}$	Y $= 1\frac{8}{15}$
E $= \frac{5}{7}$	Q $= \frac{1}{15}$	
F $= \frac{7}{12}$	R $= 1\frac{1}{10}$	
G $= \frac{5}{16}$	S $= \frac{7}{15}$	
I $= \frac{2}{5}$	T $= \frac{7}{8}$	
K $= \frac{2}{3}$	U $= 1\frac{1}{6}$	
M $= \frac{7}{20}$		

1. A box of quackers.

2. tomorrow

3. Are you putting me on?

Page 18

2. $\frac{1}{4}$ $\frac{2}{5}$ **4.** $\frac{1}{8}$ $\frac{3}{4}$ **6.** $\frac{2}{3}$ $\frac{1}{6}$

3. $\frac{2}{5}$ $\frac{1}{3}$ **5.** $\frac{1}{6}$ $\frac{5}{8}$ **7.** $\frac{1}{2}$ $\frac{3}{5}$

Page 19

Page 20

$\frac{2}{3} = 0.66$ $\frac{5}{8} = 0.63$

$\frac{3}{4} = 0.75$ $\frac{7}{9} = 0.78$

$\frac{2}{5} = 0.40$ $\frac{8}{9} = 0.89$

$\frac{5}{6} = 0.83$ $\frac{3}{10} = 0.30$

$\frac{5}{7} = 0.71$ $\frac{1}{12} = 0.08$

$\frac{6}{7} = 0.86$ $\frac{11}{12} = 0.92$

$\frac{1}{8} = 0.13$ $\frac{7}{15} = 0.46 \ (0.4666)$

$\frac{3}{8} = 0.38$ $\frac{7}{20} = 0.35$

Page 21

1. 0.026, 0.201, 0.232, 0.297, 0.321—Orion
2. 0.003, 0.013, 0.113, 0.131, 0.133, 0.333—Cygnus
3. 0.03, 0.103, 0.113, 0.312, 0.378, 0.406, 0.46, 0.705, 0.75—Big Dipper

Page 22

2. 2.45 + 1.027
3. 6.712 + 3.14
4. 1.432 + 3.789
5. 7.643 − 1.321
6. 0.962 − 0.235
7. 1.25 − 0.567
8. 6.372 − 1.027

Page 23

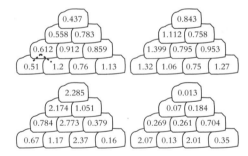

Page 24

1. 37.5%   4. 63.6%
2. 41.7%   5. 35.7%
3. 28.6%   6. 55.6%

Number 4 is the haunted mansion Gregor is looking for.

Page 25

1. $22.46   4. $41.88
2. $10.55   5. $71.22
3. $64.58   6. $81.96

Page 26

ratios equal to $\frac{2}{3}$: $\frac{6}{9}, \frac{10}{15}, \frac{12}{18}, \frac{30}{45}, \frac{36}{54}, \frac{44}{66}, \frac{24}{36}, \frac{18}{27}$

Page 27

2. 20 feet
3. 18 feet

Page 28

6: 3.7

7: 2.2

8: 1.3

9: .8

10: .5

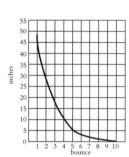

Page 29

Answers and graphs will vary depending on individual data.

Page 30

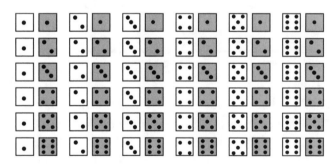

2. 4 outcomes have a total of 5.
   Probability is 4 out of 36 or 1 out of 9 chances of getting 5.
3. 6 outcomes are doubles.
   Probability is 6 out of 36 or 1 out of 6 chances of getting a double.
4. 1 outcome is a double 1.
   Probability is 1 out of 36 of getting a double 1.

Page 31

1. Kim = blue; Joan = green; Tanya = yellow; Sally = red
2. There were 3 people: a grandfather, father, and son. The father of the son was also the son of the grandfather.
3. Since August has 31 days, the lake will be half covered on August 30. One more double and the lake is entirely covered.
4. 3,647
5. $\frac{12}{18}$
6. Lou will get 10 free bags. He will get 8 free bags with the 71 labels and have 7 labels left over. Each of the 8 free bags has a label so he uses them to get his ninth free bag. With the ninth bag's labels and the 7 labels he had left over at the beginning, Lou can get his tenth bag.

Page 32

x + 1 18	x − 6 11	x − 1 16
x − 4 13	x − 2 15	x = 17 17
x − 3 14	x + 2 19	x − 5 12

Magic Number: 45

12	5	y + 4 10
y + 1 7	y + 3 9	11
y + 2 8	13	y = 6 6

Magic Number: 27

Page 33

1. Your heart beats about 100,000 times a day.
2. The temperature at the center of the sun is about 27,000,000° F.
3. The sun is about 93,000,000 miles from Earth.
4. About 250,000,000 people live in the United States.
5. Each day, about 2,000,000,000 of your body's cells are replaced.
6. Earth is about 4,500,000,000 years old.
7. About 5,770,000,000 people live in the world.
8. There are about 200,000,000,000,000,000,000,000 stars.

Page 34

1. 490
2. 21,114
3. 22,000
4. 800,000
5. 300,000
6. 14,500
7. 36,160
8. 350,000

Page 35

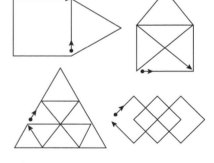

Page 36

Sample answers.

−4	+1	0
+3	−1	−5
−2	−3	+2

Page 37

1. 1 square
   1 triangle
2. 1 square
   9 triangles
3. 0 squares
   13 triangles
4. 7 squares
   0 triangles

Page 38

No answer necessary.

Page 39

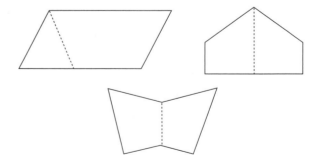

68

Grades 5 & 6

Page 40

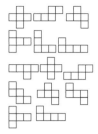

Page 41

The shape is a cube.

Page 42

Octahedron patterns

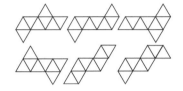

Page 43

1. b   **3.** a
2. d   **4.** c

Page 44

A. Volume: 512 cu. in.   **B.** Volume: 144 cu. in.
C. Volume: 288 cu. in.   **D.** Volume: 480 cu. in.

1. D   **3.** A
2. B   **4.** C

Page 45

1. 50.24 sq. in.   **4.** 452.16 sq. in.
2. 100.48 sq. in.   **5.** 376.8 sq. in.
3. 226.08 sq. in.   **6.** 75.36 sq. in.

Page 46

1. R $8\frac{3}{4}$ **8.** E $5\frac{1}{4}$
2. A $8\frac{5}{24}$ **9.** N $7\frac{1}{8}$
3. G $1\frac{1}{3}$ **10.** N $12\frac{7}{12}$
4. L $5\frac{1}{20}$ **11.** S $\frac{5}{12}$
5. O $4\frac{3}{4}$ **12.** R   18
6. M $7\frac{1}{4}$ **13.** I $9\frac{3}{4}$
7. T $2\frac{1}{2}$

$\underset{9}{N}\ \underset{8}{E}\ \underset{13}{I}\ \underset{4}{L}$ $\underset{2}{A}\ \underset{1}{R}\ \underset{6}{M}\ \underset{11}{S}\ \underset{7}{T}\ \underset{12}{R}\ \underset{5}{O}\ \underset{10}{N}\ \underset{3}{G}$

Page 47

2. $\frac{3}{5}$ **5.** $\frac{1}{2}$ **8.** $\frac{2}{3}$
3. $\frac{5}{8}$ **6.** $\frac{2}{3}$
4. $\frac{5}{6}$ **7.** $\frac{5}{8}$

Page 48

1. $\frac{2}{3}$ **4.** $2\frac{5}{8}$
2. $5\frac{1}{2}$ **5.** $2\frac{1}{4}$
3. $1\frac{3}{5}$ **6.** 6

Page 49

1. 2.64   **4.** 3.71
2. 17.62   **5.** 55.6
3. 4.58   **6.** 1.342

Page 50

1. $\frac{2}{9} = 0.\overline{2}; \frac{3}{9} = 0.\overline{3}; \frac{4}{9} = 0.\overline{4}; \frac{5}{9} = 0.\overline{5}; \frac{6}{9} = 0.\overline{6}$
The digits in the decimal increase by 1 each time.

2. $\frac{2}{11} = 0.\overline{18}; \frac{3}{11} = 0.\overline{27}; \frac{4}{11} = 0.\overline{36}; \frac{5}{11} = 0.\overline{45};$ $\frac{6}{11} = 0.\overline{54}$
The digit in the tenths place increases by 1 as the digit in the hundredths place decreases by 1.

3. $\frac{1}{33} = 0.\overline{03}; \frac{2}{33} = 0.\overline{06}; \frac{3}{33} = 0.\overline{09}; \frac{4}{33} = 0.\overline{12};$ $\frac{5}{33} = 0.\overline{15}; \frac{6}{33} = 0.\overline{18}$
The digit in the hundredths place increases by 3 each time.

4. $\frac{1}{99} = 0.\overline{01}; \frac{2}{99} = 0.\overline{02}; \frac{3}{99} = 0.\overline{03}; \frac{4}{99} = 0.\overline{04};$ $\frac{5}{99} = 0.\overline{05}; \frac{6}{99} = 0.\overline{06}$
The digit in the hundredths place increases by 1 each time.

Page 51

1. **b.** 5   **2. a.** 2   **3. a.** 8
   c. 6   **b.** 5   **b.** 4
   d. 4   **c.** 7   **c.** 9
   e. 9   **d.** 4   **d.** 2
   f. 8   **e.** 9   **e.** 6
               f. 3   **f.** 5

Page 52

2. 0.3 $\frac{2}{5}$ 30% **7.** 25% $\frac{3}{5}$ 0.15

3. 64% 0.26 $\frac{1}{10}$ **8.** 0.15 $\frac{9}{12}$ 10%

4. 40% 0.4 $\frac{1}{5}$ **9.** 20% 0.4 $\frac{2}{5}$

5. $\frac{1}{5}$ 50% 0.30 **10.** $\frac{1}{4}$ 0.15 60%

6. 26% $\frac{3}{5}$ 14%

Page 53

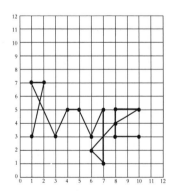

Page 54

2. seem, leak: 1 to 2
3. cooler, seek: 1 to 2
4. fast, slam: 1 to 4
5. different, listen: 1 to 3
6. moose, piano: 3 to 5
7. badge, floor: 2 to 5
8. lecture, leather: 3 to 7
9. maintain, magazine: 1 to 2
10. neighborhood, intersection: 5 to 12

Page 55

The drawing is 2 times or twice as large as the original.

Page 56

Page 57

Answers will vary.

Page 58

Winning combinations:

1, 2, 4	2, 4, 1
1, 3, 3	3, 1, 3
1, 4, 2	3, 2, 2
2, 1, 4	3, 3, 1
2, 2, 3	4, 1, 2
2, 3, 2	3, 2, 1

12 out of 64 chances of winning

Page 59

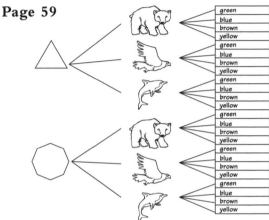

There are 24 possible outcomes.

Page 60

The 25 prime numbers left unshaded on your chart should be: 2, 3, 5, 7, 11, 13, 17, 19, 23, 29, 31, 37, 41, 43, 47, 53, 59, 61, 67, 71, 73, 79, 83, 89, 97

Page 61

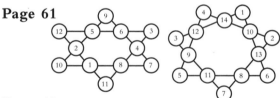

Page 62

1. 375 feet
2. The order is: Creature Comforts, Read More, Post Office, Mike's Deli.
3. Rusty was third.

Page 63

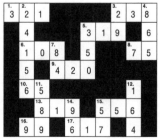

How Do You Foster Your Child's Interest in Learning?

In preparing this series, we surveyed scores of parents on this key question. Here are some of the best suggestions:

- Take weekly trips to the library to take out books, and attend special library events.

- Have lots of books around the house, especially on topics of specific interest to children.

- Read out loud nightly.

- Take turns reading to each other.

- Subscribe to age-appropriate magazines.

- Point out articles of interest in the newspaper or a magazine.

- Tell each other stories.

- Encourage children to write journal entries and short stories.

- Ask them to write letters and make cards for special occasions.

- Discuss all the things you do together.

- Limit TV time.

- Watch selected programs on TV together, like learning/educational channels.

- Provide project workbooks purchased at teacher supply stores.

- Supply lots of arts and crafts materials and encourage children to be creative.

- Encourage children to express themselves in a variety of ways.

- Take science and nature walks.

- Teach children to play challenging games such as chess.

- Provide educational board games.

- Supply lots of educational and recreational computer games.

- Discuss what children are learning and doing on a daily basis.

- Invite classmates and other friends over to your house for team homework assignments.

- Keep the learning experiences fun for children.

- Help children with their homework and class assignments.

- Take trips to museums and museum classes.

- Visits cities of historical interest.

- Takes trips to the ocean and other fun outdoor locations (fishing at lakes, mountain hikes).

- Visit the aquarium and zoo.

- Cook, bake, and measure ingredients.

- Encourage children to participate in sports.

- Listen to music, attend concerts, and encourage children to take music lessons.

- Be positive about books, trips, and other daily experiences.

- Take family walks.

- Let children be part of the family decision-making process.

- Sit down together to eat and talk.

- Give a lot of praise and positive reinforcement for your child's efforts.

- Review child's homework that has been returned by the teacher.

- Encourage children to use resources such as the dictionary, encyclopedia, thesaurus, and atlas.

- Plant a vegetable garden outdoors or in pots in your kitchen.

- Make each child in your family feel he or she is special.

- Don't allow children to give up, especially when it comes to learning and dealing with challenges.

- Instill a love of language; it will expose your child to a richer thought bank.

- Tell your children stories that share, not necessarily teach a lesson.

- Communicate your personal processes with your children.

- Don't talk about what your child did not do. Put more interest on what your child did do. Accept where your child is at, and praise his or her efforts.

- Express an interest in children's activities and schoolwork.

- Limit TV viewing time at home and foster good viewing habits.

- Work on enlarging children's vocabulary.

- Emphasize learning accomplishments, no matter how small.

- Go at their own pace; People learn at different rates.

- Challenge children to take risks.

- Encourage them to do their best, not be the best.